You Own It.
Now Grow It!

25 powerful relationship skills

effective entrepreneurs use

to grow successful businesses

by Kim Leatherdale

DEDICATION

For my mother, the epitome of an effective business person with fantastic relationship skills, thanks for teaching me so much about life and business.

Thank you!

As a thank you for purchasing my book, I would like to give you a free list *"Common Mistakes People Make in Communication."* Just go to **eepurl.com/bU_Jdj**.

Here's to good reading, wonderful skills, and a successful business!

Contents

INTRODUCTION

Whether it is in the workplace between co-workers, while interacting with vendors, or while selling to customers, business is all about relationships. To build a great business it is important that you know how to use and leverage all types of relationship skills. When you are "doing it right" those who interact with you help your business succeed and ultimately grow it to the place you want it to be. Your customers become sales people and advocates, your vendors refer to you and talk you up, and the atmosphere in the workplace is focused and happy.

In this book you will be introduced to 25 powerful relationship skills you can use to successfully grow your business. I will describe each skill, explain why it is important in your business, give examples, and challenge you to implement each one. When practiced correctly, these skills will help you cultivate a great business.

Who am I to tell you about relationship skills in business? First of all I am a successful business owner with a leg up on all these skills - I teach them in my practice. As a coach and counselor, I am constantly helping clients create the type of relationships they would like in their personal and professional lives.

Secondly, I practice the things I teach; that's how I became a successful business person. Unlike many counselors, I have never accepted insurance as an easy marketing tool (and a pain in the butt reimbursement provider); I marketed my own practice. Hitting the streets and the networking groups to find clients, I quickly learned the importance of these relationship skills in growing my practice. I found the business people in my networking groups were hungry to understand them, too, and talked to me incessantly about them. Thus the idea for this book was born.

The best thing about this book is you can use each skill immediately and see changes in your business success in a very short time. Additionally, these skills are transferable to all areas of your life.

Don't miss out on this opportunity to improve the most important skills of your life and business – powerful relationship skills. Be the kind of entrepreneur who other people marvel at. Be that person others see and say, "Wow, they really know people." Be the person who takes action and does so immediately to improve their business.

How to use this book:

- Please read it - don't just skim the beginnings of each chapter and skip them because think you know what I'm going to say. I suspect I'll say things you won't expect. Read and internalize the information I share. Take time to mull over the questions at the end of each chapter so you can assimilate the information you have taken the time to read. Use the extra space around the text and the lines after the questions to jot down thoughts and inspirations.
- Get a journal and write down your answers. There is a power in putting words onto paper rather than just bouncing them around in your head. One big plus will be your ability to see patterns emerge as you do each section.
- Put the skills you read about into practice, and treat them like practice. I guarantee you won't do things perfectly the first time or the tenth time; that's why it is called practice. However, the more you do each skill, the better you will be at them and the bigger your return. Use these skills in *all* areas of your life, not just work. Apply what you learn and live it.

- Lastly, share this book with friends, colleagues, bosses, mentees, family members, and anyone you think could use it. My plan is to keep this book reasonably priced because I would love to see more businesses using healthy relationship skills. Encourage others to buy, read, and pass it along. I'm hoping this book is like the proverbial pebble in the pond rippling out to improve every business and life it touches.

The skills outlined in this book have great power to grow your business. I hope you use that power for the good of not only your business, but your customers, clients and the world. The best thing you can do to start improving all three is turn the page and start reading. Now.

Let's drop the first pebble in the pond and start with communication skills.

Communication is Core

Communication is at the core of every good relationship. It informs every interaction and is what both people take away at the end of every contact. How you communicate with your customer will make or break your sales and seriously impact your reputation. How you communicate with your co-workers, employees, or boss will determine how happy and productive you are in your workplace. How you communicate with vendors will help or hamper how you receive products and services.

Communication is multi-faceted. It involves transmission and reception. You communicate both verbally and non-verbally. And let us not forget how often we communicate via technology these days. All these things need to be taken into consideration to be merely good at communication. It takes added skills and techniques to be great at communication in business relationships.

Let's start with a basic premise that good communication takes two.

It takes a speaker *and* a listener for good communication. It takes transmission and reception. It means **both** ears and mouth must be working correctly. When there are problems in communication the speaker may be off, the listener may be off, or both may be off. For relationship health and business success both must be **on**.

However, too many people have no idea what to **do** when they are in either of these roles; therefore, ***communication fails!***

Let's look at the actual responsibilities associated with each role. I'll be fleshing these out in the next chapters, but let's get an overview of how they fit into the whole.

Speaker:
- asks permission to speak (makes sure the timing is right)

- speaks to be understood
- speaks without judgment
- makes a request (asks for something – for example a sale)
- keeps it simple and short (KISS)
- clarifies when asked

Listener:
- avoids talking in their head
- focuses on the speaker
- is in the service of the speaker
- listens to *understand*
- negotiates with skill- giving what they can

Both:
- practice healthy self-esteem
- hold healthy boundaries
- have the goal of connection and understanding

It looks simple, but people don't seem to be able to do only **one** of these two things. They speak when they are the listener, and they forget their role responsibilities. They fall off the communication wagon.

For example (names changed to protect the not so innocent):

1. Sue is so mad at her boss she speaks in a sarcastic tone
2. Bob thinks about other things while his business partner is talking to him.
3. Barb barges in and tells her coworker "We *have* to talk **now**."
4. Tom shames his peer repeatedly with phrases like "you're just too sensitive," or "you work yourself up too much."
5. Laura can't wait for her employee to take a breath so she can jump in and tell him the true version of things.
6. Brad argues about what he can't do when his boss makes a request.

7. Fran repeatedly complains about things her vendor does wrong, but doesn't specifically ask him to do something differently (or say what she does want.)
8. John rambles on and on about a variety of different things and often diverges completely from the beginning of the conversation.

*Do **you** recognize yourself in any of the above?* **Stop**.

Each person has forgotten their role.

Speakers:

- Sue (1) and Tom (4) have poor boundaries and are being judgmental.
- Barb (3) isn't showing respect for her coworker's time or needs.
- Fran (7) isn't talking about her needs or making specific requests.
- John (8) needs to learn the definition of succinct.

Listeners:
- Bob (2) and Laura (5) aren't really listening or focusing.
- Brad (6) needs to learn how to negotiate with skill and thought.

Practicing the skills of both speaking and listening will move your business into a fantastic place no matter what your personal and professional differences with others may be.

Here are the listening skills we are going to cover that can raise your business to the next level.

- Why you listen
- How you show you listened
- How and when to ask questions

Skill #1 – Listen to Understand

Most professionals have heard the recommendation on listening which encourages them to stop the chatter in their head, to focus on the speaker, but they often miss the primary mission of listening. **Why** you listen.

Real listening is about understanding the speaker.

Many people (in both their personal and professional lives) forget understanding is their job when they listen. They get caught up in who is "right" or waiting to correct the other person. They are stuck in the chatter, but even more so, they are missing out on great information they could be getting.

Why is it important to understand when you listen? Because you can learn so much. If you are in sales, you can learn the underlying needs and wants of your customer, not just the surface verbiage. If you are a boss, you can understand the thinking and needs of your employees. If you are a business owner, you can understand the marketplace and make sure you are putting yourself where people are looking.

Good listening is solely about understanding the other person. It is not about correcting them, defending yourself, or even agreeing with them. Just "get" what they think, feel, and want. You have to step aside from your own thoughts and hear theirs.

When your customer, vendor, coworker or boss is speaking to you, does your internal dialogue sound something like the following?

"Oh, how can she say that?!...
"I've got to straighten him out on that point....
"That's just downright wrong!...
"She doesn't understand...
"Right, I need to explain to him about that!...
"How can she be so confused?...

"Is he still talking?...
"I've got to remember to tell her this..."
And so on. (By the way, these mental comments can be set aside to use when you clarify- see the later chapter on clarifying)

You may even have a moment of "Oh, look, a butterfly!.... Now, what was he saying?"

If any of that sounds familiar, *you really aren't listening*. Yes, you are hearing words, but you aren't listening. You are talking and arguing in your head. At that moment there are **two** speakers and **no** listener. This is not a good recipe for communication.

So, how should your internal dialogue really sound while listening?

First, it will be primarily quiet since you are *focused on* the speaker. You shouldn't be doing *any* talking about your own story, even in your head.

Now you might hear these phrases:

"Oh, interesting, I didn't realize she felt that way...."
"I'm not sure I understand that, I need to ask him about it...."
"Okay, I think I have it, but I'll keep listening to make sure...."

Your whole attention is on what is being said and what is meant.

As the listener **you are working to understand, not to be understood**. So your inner speaker needs to be silent except when it comes to curiosity and clarification. Your turn to speak and be understood *only* comes *after* you have passed the test as the listener- **to understand** (not agree, not sell, not believe, not convince, not change someone's mind, not explain, etc.)

Thoughtful Questions:

What are the mistakes you most often make while listening?

_____

_____

_____

_____

What beliefs drive those mistakes?

_____

_____

_____

_____

What do you think about when listening to someone?

_____

_____

_____

_____

What problems have you had due to not listening to understand?

_____

_____

_____

_____

How do you think people will respond when you are listening to understand?

_____

_____

_____

_____

How do you think focusing on understanding will change your business relationships?

_____

_____

_____

_____

What do you believe will be the most challenging part of listening to understand?

_____

_____

_____

_____

Skillful Practice:

Choose one discussion in the next 24-48 hours where you put yourself aside and focus on listening to understand the other person. See how well you do, be aware of any changes in dynamics that happen from this new focus, recognize if understanding improves something, and check out your own resistances to listening this way. Jot down notes in your journal (or below) on how it was to listen to understand.

Skill #2 - SHOW you understand

When business people listen they often focus on the bottom line – what it is they need to *do* and how can they make the sale or fix a problem in the workplace. Do you do this? Do you jump immediately to a solution or what should be changed? Do you agree to requests and offer the ways you can help? And aren't you confused and upset when your boss or coworker (or even customer) still isn't happy?

Actually those people *shouldn't* be happy because they are not being heard.

Why? Because you didn't express a full understanding *of the speaker*. You grasped the request, but you did not get where the speaker is at. You left out the step of paraphrasing to express understanding.

Believe me, in the moment **showing you comprehend the speaker is more important than fixing the problem or offering to help.** Teddy Roosevelt said best when he said, *"People don't care how much you know until they know how much you care."*

For those who are focused on solution – *the first step in any solution is to* **understand** *the person talking to you.* We say this about customers - learn what they are feeling and you can offer them what they want or need. The same holds true with your coworker or boss. You need to value where they are coming from before you try to fix anything.

Besides, without showing your full understanding, you can't check if you are right. The speaker gets no chance to clarify if you are off. And then you may go on to correct something that didn't need addressing or incorrectly addressing what they are struggling with. If you jump directly to the request or "what will fix this" the other person may think you are only interested in "getting it over with" and if that is where you are at, it still is bad business to give that impression.

How do you show you understood? You paraphrase (not parrot) what you just heard. You say "Let me see if I got this right" and go on to share what you think the person just said. All of what they said – what bothered them, how they felt, what their frustrations or needs are, what they think the problem is, and what they are asking for. Don't skip any part of what they shared. And then you ask "Did I understand you correctly?"

They want to know that you "got" them; that you understand and know where they are coming from. That way they know you are going to give them the help, product, solutions, and directions that will fit them, and not use a cookie cutter approach.

Here's the main principle of listening: understand in the moment your boss, coworker, vendor, or customer doesn't give a fig about your issues; *what they want to know right now is you are interested in them.*

Then, and only then, will you move to solution and agreement.

> *"The only factor becoming scarce*
> *in a world of abundance*
> *is human attention."*
> -Kevin Kelly

A few mistakes are often made in understanding:

1. Instead of understanding and paraphrasing you defend yourself or your interpretation of events.
2. You tune out and miss parts that are important to the speaker.
3. You focus on small parts of the information rather than the whole tale.
4. You wait for the end rather than focusing on the meaning.

5. You interrupt and don't get the whole story.
6. You look only for solution.

This is not communication, it is not connection, and it isn't good business sense. People want to do business with professionals who connect, not dismiss.

Here's what those mistakes do:

1. By defending yourself you have become a speaker and failed in your job of understanding.
2. If you interrupt before the speaker is done you appear self-centered. ***When you agreed to listen, you put yourself in the speaker's service.***
3. By not looking at the whole story *you imply you don't care* enough about the speaker to truly pay attention to what they are saying. With customers, employees, and vendors this is devastating to your retention rate.

So, show the speaker you understand. Paraphrase the concerns you heard your customer voice before you attempt to address them. Make sure you heard your employee correctly when they asked something of you by reviewing what they said. Make clear the expectations a vendor may have by spelling them out again. Paraphrasing your understanding is not a waste of time; it ultimately will save you time by short circuiting business misunderstandings.

Thoughtful Questions:

What are the mistakes you most often make while paraphrasing?

_____

_____

_____

_____

What automatic internal thoughts drive those mistakes?

_____

_____

_____

_____

What assumptions do you make which are damaging your ability
to paraphrase?

_____

_____

_____

_____

What problems have you had due to not paraphrasing?

_____

_____

_____

_____

How do you think people will respond when you paraphrase?

_____

_____

_____

_____

How do you think paraphrasing could change your business relationships?

_____

_____

_____

_____

How could it improve your business overall?

_____

_____

_____

_____

What do you believe will be the most challenging part of paraphrasing?

_____

_____

_____

_____

Skillful Practice:

Before responding to what someone says, take a moment to paraphrase what you heard. Check with the other person to see if you "got it." Pay attention to the assumptions you make and where you are most often wrong or missing information. Use this to brush up on your understanding and paraphrasing skills. Use your journal to take notes on the impact paraphrasing seems to have on discussions and interactions.

Skill #3 - Clarify curiously

One healthy listening skill is *asking questions to clarify* what was said by your coworker, vendor, boss, or customer. As a listener your job is to focus on understanding the other person, not defend your ideas or intentions. So, if you are not sure of something that was said, ask a question to clarify the information.

Remember we discussed how your mind will come up with questions like:

- "Oh, how can she say that?!...
- "What is he getting at?
- "How can she be so confused?...
- "Is he still talking?...
- "I've got to remember to tell him/her this..."

Those questions indicate the areas where you may be unclear or confused. These are the issues where you want to clarify and curiously inquire.

What makes the questions work is the **tone** you use while asking them. It is important you are *curious* in your questions so they don't come across as judgmental or attacking. If you remember your role is to understand, you'll be less likely to get defensive.

(Interesting side note: studies have shown men are less likely to ask questions for fear of seeming unintelligent. However, men, by not asking questions, you may give your customers and peers the impression you don't care. Ask away!)

In all interactions focus on a sense of curiosity rather than an air of confrontation.

Do you find yourself slipping into listening for "mistakes" when someone is talking? You tally those mistakes up and when they are done, you pounce on their argument, ripping it to shreds! Or, you ask questions like, "Why in the world did you do that?" or "How could you think that?" Or your tone implies they are wrong, stupid, or just plain confused. Or your mind insists you are right and they are wrong even if you don' t say it. Or you have been accused of having a judgmental attitude by coworkers, on reviews, or by people you know.

I could go on, but I hope you get the picture.

We learn from an early age (especially men) to compete with others, to defend what is "right" (in our eyes) and to come out on top. Tell me this isn't so!

The problem is, a competitive attitude kills relationships, and good relationships are what will help you do great business.

What you need to do is **replace competition with a sense of curiosity**. How?

- When someone is talking, listen and try to understand (not see if they are "right".)

- If you don't understand something, ask about it (not fight about it.)

- Remember this is their reality/understanding of the situation, and you don't have to agree, just respect that it belongs to them.

- Avoid "why" questions (they come across as judgmental.) Rephrase.

- Forget who is right or wrong and focus on connecting, understanding, and moving forward.

- Use a tone of question rather than censure.

When you are curious rather than confrontational, people are more likely to want to work with you. They will work hard to come to understanding and make themselves clear. With curious clarification you build a business where respect is primary and harmony more likely. It also helps your business in times of conflict (which I'll address later in this book), by creating an atmosphere of trust. Be curious, be open, ask questions, and be rewarded with business success.

Thoughtful Questions:

What do you believe will be the most challenging part of clarifying in a curious fashion?

_____

_____

_____

_____

What are the mistakes you most often make while asking questions?

_____

_____

_____

_____

Have you ever been told your tone is problematic? What have you done when given that feedback?

_____

_____

_____

_____

What problems have you had due to your tone?

_____

_____

_____

_____

How have you responded to questions about your ideas in the past?

_____

_____

_____

_____

How have you responded to curiosity in the workplace? Do you encourage it in others? Have you ever experienced censure for curiosity?

_____

_____

_____

_____

How do you think people will respond when you are curious rather than confrontational?

_____

_____

_____

_____

How do you think focusing on curiosity will change your business relationships?

_____

_____

_____

_____

Skillful Practice:

When you are tempted to challenge someone about what they said, take a breath and ask them a few questions in a curious fashion. Focus on getting them (listening to understand) and seeing their inner ideas. Rather than attacking, ask questions, slow down and listen. If you don't agree afterward, paraphrase what you heard, and only then respectfully disagree. Jot down your experiences with curious clarification.

Introducing the speaking skills

Despite all the time we spend talking most people don't know how to skillfully share ideas, troubles, and thoughts. Speaking is a skill most business people could stand to polish; however, most mistakenly believe they already do this part well.

One problem is we spend too much time speaking. We speak in our heads, we speak on the phone, we speak on social media, we speak to ourselves, we speak to sell, we speak to start a deal, we speak to close a deal; we speak constantly! And all this speaking makes us feel we must be good at it.

Practice doesn't make perfect if you are practicing badly. You are just making yourself perfect at the bad habits.

Let's look at a few healthy habits you can practice in your speaking. We're going to cover:

- How conviction isn't communication
- "Why" you speak is paramount
- When making a request is business savvy
- Speaking to create great business associates
- Obstacles to direction giving and taking
- The importance of "but-ing" out

Skill #4 - Don't Be Barry

A client shared a gem she heard from a personal coach:

"When you state things with conviction you destroy all chance of conversation."

Let that sink in for a moment.

If you state something as if it were *the only truth and the only way*, are you opening up conversation? No, if you speak like this, you give the impression to others you can't be spoken to about other options or ideas. At work this creates an image of you as inflexible. If you speak this way with customers, coworkers or employees, you shut them down.

A shut down business associate isn't going to feel very comfortable or happy with you. They are probably going to be pretty put-off. In interactions where you are looking for feedback and ideas, you are going to miss out.

The fact is you can be solid in your truths or understandings without negating what someone else thinks or believes. This is done with tactful honest communication.

Let me give you an example. I have a friend who is unafraid to tell people what she thinks, including giving people "helpful suggestions" regularly. Her ideas are sound, but the way she delivers them leaves much to be desired. She says things like: "You should..." and "The best way is..." and "I've always read the smart thing to do is...."

See what I'm getting at? She is giving the person she is "helping" no options- if they do something differently they are bad, stupid, or not smart.

How could she say things differently but still give her advice? Tactful caring communication; for example, "What I've found helpful sometimes is to..." or "One way to do it is..." or "A way I've heard of is...." These are all offering options, but not touting them as "the best", "smartest" or "only" ways. She would be choosing words that make it clear they are only ideas and not judgments.

Of course, this skill is about business relationships where you aren't responsible for determining and enforcing policy. In a healthy business, policy is delivered in a caring rather than totalitarian way.

It's not only about word choice; this skill is about "*how*" you say it. Tone of voice should be open, light, and considerate; not stern, curt, or intense. It should leave the other person with the impression discussion is accepted and even expected. It definitely helps if you remind yourself you are just *offering*, not pushing, your ideas. You may consider delivering your ideas with a small smile to keep your voice and tone happier. You tell yourself and your business associate, "I'm interested in your ideas, too."

Your goal is to create an open, sharing relationship which is a ground for true connection and partnership. Barry had trouble with this; let me present the story of Barry to nail down the importance of presentation in your business.

I recently read a great short story by George Alec Effinger called "*The Aliens Who Knew, I Mean, Everything.*" It's about a group of friendly aliens who come to Earth and help humans establish world peace, end poverty, etc., but it is the way they do it which is the kicker. I won't spoil the storyline, read it yourself.

However, I do wish to talk about one character in the story, Barry. I'll let the author explain:

"Barry was a wealth of information.
He was the campus arbiter of good taste.
Everyone knew Barry was the man to ask.
But no one ever did. We all hated his guts."

Barry told everyone who the best artist was, what food and drink to order at a restaurant, what made a good or bad president, what pet everyone should have, what books were worth reading… you get the picture. "To Barry, the world was divided into masterpieces and abominations…. He never understood why his friends could never tell one from the other."

Barry makes for funny reading, but his plight is serious.

You see, Barry is stuck in being right rather than being relational. He knows what is best, he's going to tell everyone with conviction, and doesn't understand why others don't agree with him. Isn't his way best? Aren't his arguments clear? Maybe, but everyone still hates his guts.

Why? Because Barry doesn't listen, he sticks to **his** truth as if it was **_The_ Truth,** and misses the rest of the world.

Barry is an extreme example, but have you ever stuck to your truth and refused to hear from a business associate? You may have negated your coworker's arguments as "irrational" or "overly emotional." You may have felt if you could "just get them to listen and understand they'd see it my way."

Yep, you were Barry.

I fell into this trap right out of college. It was my first job, and I was full of excitement about what I was doing, what I learned in school, and how things are "supposed" to work in treatment. I wasn't shy about sharing this information, and I did so in an excited happy way. One day, Bobby, the head nurse, took me aside and shared a revelation with me. "Kim," she said, "all of these nurses have been doing this for a long time. We understand you have great intentions, but you need to stop telling us how to do our jobs."

It hit me then; I was *telling* people what they should be doing, even when I was making nice "suggestions" (repeatedly). I had not asked them why they were doing things the way they did. I had not respected their experience and knowledge. I was lucky to have Bobby; she could help me see my mistake before I drove my co-workers away. It was an important lesson that stuck through the years.

The lesson? *Being right drives people away. Being relational keeps them around.*

Thoughtful Questions:

Have you ever fallen into the habit of speaking as if there was only one way?

_____

_____

_____

_____

Who do you know that speaks with conviction in such a way that closes off conversation? How is it to interact with that person?

_____

_____

_____

_____

Are there places or responsibilities where you do this more?

_____
_____
_____
_____

Do you do it at home?

_____
_____
_____
_____

Have you changed it?

_____
_____
_____
_____

Who do you know who "knows everything"?

_____
_____
_____
_____

How have you dealt with them?

_____

_____

_____

_____

Skillful Practice:

When you are tempted to "be the expert" on something, consider your phrasing. You may have a great idea, and you can present it as "a great idea" not "this is what we should do." Focus on opening up discussion rather than presenting "the best idea" in a way that shuts others down. Use phrases like "How about we consider" and "This could work; what do you think?" Jot down your experiences with being less like Barry and more like a responsive open business person.

Skill #5 - Speak to be understood

One difficulty many people have in business is giving negative feedback or constructive criticism. They forget feedback is about helping the other person. It is about coming to understanding and clarity. It is a chance for repair. There are a few steps you can take to make giving recommendations or even criticism go more smoothly.

The first thing you must do is chose an appropriate time and ask for a chance to speak with the business associate. It is important you respect the person enough to ask if they have time and inclination. The request can look like: "I have some feedback about something going on, would you hear it?"

When the person is ready, *give your information in the following manner:*

1. **State an observable behavior** (as a video could record it, no judgment or interpretation)
—*"When you came into work late three times last week..."*
2. **Share how you interpreted it** (the thoughts you had)
—*"I imagined you have lost interest in your work..."*
3. **Share how this impacts the business relationship** (keep it simple)
— *"Losing your time impacts the start of meetings..."*
4. **Ask for what you would like** (make a request- without this you are only complaining)
— *"We need to discuss if your hours should change so that you can get to work on time"* or *"Please let me know if something is going on which might make you late so I can reschedule meetings."* (More on this in the next chapter.)

Hints:

- Be clear you are speaking about your reality, not the "truth". They may be interested in work, but had sick family members this week.
- Always focus on the request, not complaint- speaking is about connecting!
- You get more of what you want by asking, not pointing out what the person is doing wrong.
- When your employee agrees to do something, show gratitude; say "thank you."
- Ask what you can do to help the person do the things you asked for.
- When they do what you asked, appreciate it.
- Avoid disqualifying when the person does what you ask; e.g. don't say "You're just doing it because I asked" or "You don't really mean it" or "That's easy to do."

As you speak to be understood, it will encourage your clarity and directness. You will become better at business interactions because you will pay attention to how best to help the other person understand what you are saying. You will also find more things are accomplished as you clearly state your need through a request. All of this will build your business quickly.

Thoughtful Questions:

What do you believe will be the most challenging part of speaking to be understood?

_____

_____

_____

_____

What are the mistakes you most often make while trying to be understood or making requests?

_____

_____

_____

_____

What behavioral habits drive those mistakes?

_____

_____

_____

_____

What assumptions do you make which are damaging your ability to be understood?

_____

_____

_____

_____

How do you think people will respond when you speak to be understood? When you make a request?

_____

_____

_____

_____

How do you think speaking this way could change your business relationships?

_____

_____

_____

_____

How could speaking to be understood and making a request improve your business?

_____

_____

_____

_____

Skillful Practice:

For the next two days pay attention to how you speak to others. Do you speak to be understood or for some other reason (e.g. to hear yourself talk, to show your expertise, to fill a silence – see the later chapter on silence)? For the next three days, after paying heed to what keeps you back, focus on really speaking to be understood. Concentrate on how you speak to each person so that they really get what you are saying. Make sure you are speaking in a way they can hear you. And once you know they have heard you, make your request. Journal your thoughts and experiences.

Skill #6 - Make a request

Those who thrive in business clearly understand one rule – they ask for things. In particular, they ask for actions. They ask for a sale from customers, they ask for great service from vendors, they ask for specific behaviors from their employees. They make clear to others what they are looking for.

This means the savvy business person makes a request when speaking. It doesn't always have to be a specific action, but you need to give the listener a chance to do something with what you shared. While you are sharing so someone understands your thoughts and feelings, you also need to make your goal clear. If you'd like a change, ask for it. If you'd like them to buy something, say so. If you want a particular action, state it.

Often my clients complain that, even though they ask for things from others, those things aren't done. When I dig deeper I learn the reason – the requests aren't specific enough.

You may say something like:

1. I want my customer to be supportive of me.

2. I want my employee to show interest in the job/company.

3. I want my boss to get out of my way

4. I want my manager to provide me with challenges.

But if you say those statements generally (as written above), **the other person doesn't know what you mean**. You need to be specific and give examples.

This is where the communication collapses. You make a request of your customer; "I need your support." Your customers are supportive by encouraging you verbally in the new endeavor you are taking on. They like your posts on Facebook. They ask how things are going.

They think they are being supportive! You don't.

You have to let them know what "support" means to you. "Hey what I need from you is _____ ." E.g. "buy products", "tell your friends about my business," "write a recommendation on LinkedIn," "Review my book on Amazon." You can give them multiple options; however, if you want something particular like the recommendation, say so. "What would really help me is if you'd write a recommendation for me on LinkedIn."

[So, I'm asking you, if you like what you've read so far, go to Amazon now and post a review. You can always edit it later if you decide you want to add to it.]

You need to tell your employee what "interest in the company" looks like to you. Don't expect them to read your mind. Don't say to yourself, "If he really cared about the job/company he would know what I want." They might care, but they don't read minds. They have to learn what you want and you have to say it!

It helps if you conceptualize your request in the SMART format. Like goals, your request should be **S**pecific, **M**easurable, **A**ttainable, **R**elevant, and **T**ime bound. When you make your request fit those specifications it is easier for the other person to understand and do what you ask.

The business contact will have to hear your request more than once. When you were a kid you learned through repetition. Remember when you learned multiplication? Unless you were a savant, a math genius, or my husband you didn't learn them the first time you heard them. You had to do flash cards, reread the tables, or practice them. The same happens with your business contacts (and you) when you learn something new. So repeat your request in multiple ways.

It is important to make clear requests with all business relationships, especially with superiors.

Let's approach how to make requests of your manager/owner/director/administrator/board member (hereafter referred to as "superior" due only to their job positioning.) Most likely you aren't going to say to any of them "You need to get out of my way" or "You are too timid and don't give me enough challenges." However, you might want one of those two things, and it is still important to let your superior know that fact clearly.

In general, your superior wants you to do well because it reflects well on them. It is beyond the scope of this book to address truly difficult or extreme superiors, but let's see how you can help your superior understand what you believe will make you both shine.

You'll first have to do a little listening (hopefully you paid attention in the first few sections of the book) to understand what your superior really wants. Then tailor your requests to address those needs while expressing yours.

- If your superior wishes to look good to their boss (which most people want) then you need to express your wants in relation to that. You might say "I appreciate how important this project is to both of us, and I am committed to it. If you can step back and meet with me once a week instead of daily, I promise to use that time to make this project stellar."
- If they want to make money or get more customers, you have to show how what you are asking for will do that. You might say "I'd like to run an idea past you. When I do ____, it seems to attract more customers. Do you think you could help me do that by _____?"

- If they need to build the business, you have to express how your wants will build or improve the business. You might say "I need your help in streamlining procedures so they can be ramped up. I think if you were able to _____ it would help me make that happen."

Extra tip – Use the word "help" when making a request. People are more likely to say yes when they feel like they are *choosing* to help rather than being *told* what to do.

Business people who succeed know how to make clear and specific requests. And they aren't afraid to put them out there.

Thoughtful Questions:

What requests are easy for you to make of others in business?

_____

_____

_____

_____

What do you struggle in asking for? How are these difficult things different than the easy things?

_____

_____

_____

_____

What problems have you had due to not making requests?

_____

_____

_____

_____

What will be most difficult for you about making requests? (e.g. knowing what to ask for, knowing how to ask for it, opening up to actually ask)

_____

_____

_____

_____

How do you respond when others make requests of you?

_____

_____

_____

_____

What thoughts or expectations about asking for something hold you back from asking?

_____

_____

_____

_____

How could you make your requests more specific?

_____

_____

_____

_____

Skillful Practice:

Review how you make requests in your business. What are the things you want which you are hesitant to ask for? Identify why you don't ask. Identify at least five areas where you can make a request. For example, do you have clear call to actions on all your media? (That is a definite request!) Think of three things you could ask your customers for to help your business. Reach out to a dozen customers and ask them for one of those things. Or think of a dozen professionals you trust to be supportive, and ask them for something to assist your business (like a LinkedIn recommendation, a testimonial, a link from their webpage to yours, or what you determine would be helpful.)

Skill #7 - Create a Great Customer

From the very first interaction with a potential customer you are setting expectations. By the way you act and what you tell them, you create the type of customer they will be; you open up the possibilities. This is a terrific opportunity to determine the customers you have by how you prepare them.

The good news is by telling people what makes a successful customer you can create a great customer who will become an advocate. Additionally, if they aren't right for you, they will not become a customer. The bad news is if you flub this step you can create a drain on your business. You need to spend time grooming your customer-to-be in what are "successful" behaviors for them (and you.)

When you do this you have to make sure to bring them along with you. Have you ever noticed the following interesting phenomena on an interstate? Picture yourself riding behind someone in the right lane. You slowly creep up because they are going a few miles an hour slower than you. When you get close you turn on your left indicator and move over to pass them. You've been getting closer, it is obvious you are going faster, then something interesting happens – *they speed up and match your speed!* (Irritating isn't it?) Let's replay that scene, but this time you are briskly approaching someone from behind, you go into the left lane and quickly pass them. They may speed up a little, but because your speed is so different you pass them and outstrip them.

Ever noticed that? This is a great metaphor for your communication with a potential customer.

Simply said, if you blow by your customer with information and intensity, they may *try* to catch up, but they will be lost quickly. If you choose instead to match their speed and encourage them to come along with you they will be able to follow your ideas. In other words, **bring the other person with you**.

This was a concept drilled into my head while training to work with couples. "Take them with you" the instructor would insist. What he meant was don't assume my clients "get it" and move forward. Check with them, work with them, lay it out in stages, tell a story – make sure they understand and come along. Use better communication skills.

You can do a few simple things to make sure you and your listener are "matching speeds" so you both understand what is going on. Here are some ways to not leave your customer behind:

1. **Keep it simply simple** (KISS)- stick to one topic, one example, one event and work that one out before adding anything else. Also, talk for only a sentence or two before asking if your customer understands. If you talk for five minutes before checking, you have left them behind, guaranteed!

2. **Check in regularly**– make sure your customer is hearing what you think you are saying. I ask my clients, "What did you just hear me say?" to see if I communicated it clearly or left them eating my dust. Just because I know what I'm saying doesn't mean they get it; same goes for your customer.

3. **Tell your story**– It helps to string things together like a story. Don't jump around, keep it contiguous and clear. If you are describing an event, start at the beginning and go to the end. It is helpful to tell the story of how you got to the thought you have now. Remember, you've been thinking about whatever you are sharing, they probably haven't been.

4. **Use healthy speaking skills**– you'll definitely leave them behind if you become judgmental or impatient. Review skills on speaking earlier in this book.

5. **Be open to questions** – Don't assume that because you understand what you are saying, your customer gets it. Be open and accepting of clarifying curious questions.

You are always trying to match speeds - not just when you are speaking, but when you are listening to business associates and customers. Here are a few things you can do:

1. **Pay attention**– It is important to focus. If you find your attention wandering, bring it gently back. If you seriously miss things, let the other person know and ask them to repeat.

2. **Help them keep it simple**– If the other person is talking for a long time and you are feeling overwhelmed, ask for a break so you can let them know what you heard so far.

3. **Be curious**– An attitude of curiosity ("I'm curious what they want me to know") will help you not be defensive. When you are not defensive you can keep up.

4. **Work to understand**– If you are trying to agree, or thinking how you'll "straighten them out" you are already left behind. Your only job is to keep up so you can understand them. (See the Listening to Understand skill at the beginning of this book.)

If you use these techniques in an open and honest way you'll be more likely to have matching conversations instead of feeling like you are driving very different speeds. You will bring your customer along to the point you want them to be - with you.

Thoughtful Questions:

What do you want your customers to most understand about being your customer?

_____

_____

_____

_____

What makes a good customer to you?

_____

_____

_____

_____

Have you expressed these ideals to your clients? Do you have them outlined in a clear way on your website? In your marketing? In your head?

_____

_____

_____

_____

What can help you "slow down" so your customers can keep up with you?

_____

_____

_____

_____

Skillful Practice:

Take a piece of paper and write "Great Customer" at the top. Set a timer for ten minutes and write every word, phrase, or thought that comes to mind when you think "great customer." Push to write the whole ten minutes; it's when it gets tough that you learn important and often surprising things. Use those words to create a few catch phrases you can draw on regularly with clients. Create a story about your ideal client, your most successful client which you can share with customers as well as potential referral sources. When you share, make sure your audience is "keeping up with you" by keeping it simple, checking in, and asking for questions.

Skill #8 - Giving & Taking Directions

Have you ever been camping?

If you have ever had to erect a tent while the light was falling and you were tired, you are quite aware of the importance of directions; especially if someone was helping you. Giving directions is important in many business roles. If you are an owner/boss talking to employees, or a sales person explaining how to use a product, you have to be careful with your directions.

Here is a little fun project for you to do and see how good you are at following directions!

First, go get a piece of paper and a pen/pencil.

Go on, I'll wait......

Got it? Don't skip this step; get that paper and pencil. I promise this will be useful.

Now here are your directions:

HOW TO FOLLOW INSTRUCTIONS

1. Read everything before doing anything, but **WORK AS RAPIDLY AS YOU CAN**
2. Put your name in the upper right-hand corner of the paper, last name first.
3. Write and Circle the word "Name".
4. Write and Underline the words "right-hand" on the right-hand side of your paper.
5. Now draw a circle around the paper.
6. Sign your name under the top of the circle.
7. Draw a circle around the middle letter of your name.

8. Write the name of your state.

9. Underline all of the vowels in the name of your state.

10. Draw an 'x' in the lower left-hand corner of the paper.

11. Draw a circle around the "x" you just drew.

12. Write the name of your city.

13. Cross out the 'x" in the lower left-hand corner of your paper.

14. Speak out loud your first name when get to this point.

15. If you think you have followed instructions to this point, call out "I have" (with gusto!)

16. Count out loud, in your normal tone of voice, backwards ten to one.

17. Close your eyes and raise your left hand over your head.

18. Write your occupation in the center of the page.

19. Now that you have read the instructions carefully, do only what sentences one and three ask you to do. Ignore all other directions.

What went wrong?!

First, I hope you had a laugh. Feel free to spring this little "test" on your friends, family, kids, coworkers, employees — make sure they have a sense of humor, though.

Directions are just a form of communication. They involve both speaking and listening. Like any form of communication, they are open to misinterpretation and misunderstandings. If you don't listen (or read) closely, you can veer off down the wrong path.

How directions are given is important; how you speak and what you emphasize can impact results. If you notice, I capitalized and bolded "work as rapidly as you can." This may have contributed to your doing a bunch of things you didn't need to do (and laughing, hopefully.)

Keep an eye on how you give and take directions in your business and with customers. Use clarification (review "Clarify Curiously" earlier in the book) to ensure you got the directions. Additionally, ask those who you give directions to what they heard. This is a great way to make sure you were clear in what you said, and you won't lose business and money by heading off in the wrong direction.

Thoughtful Questions:

How are you at taking directions?

_____

_____

_____

_____

Do you listen all the way through, or fade off imagining what you need to do before the other person finishes?

_____

_____

_____

_____

When have missed directions caused problems for you? At work? At home?

_____

_____

_____

_____

Who do you have the most trouble giving directions to? What subjects do you struggle to give directions about? Why? How could you improve both/either?

_____

_____

_____

_____

Who do you have trouble taking directions from? Why? How could you improve?

_____

_____

_____

_____

Skillful Practice:

Take a look at where in your business you give directions. How clear are they? If you didn't know your product or business, could you follow them? Now simplify those directions into less than ten steps. If your directions are too wordy, people will skip over them. Reread your new directions as if you know nothing about your business; clarify and simplify more if you need to. Lastly, when giving verbal directions, make sure you take the person with you (see previous skill!)

Skill #9 - Consider Word Choices

Most business people would agree how you say something is important. It's not what you say it's how you say it, your attitude. Yes, that's true, and I don't want to give you the wrong impression. **What** you say is very important too.

The words you speak and think with create the type of world you live in. The words you use in speaking create a tone, a mood, and a story that you buy into. The ideas you have in your head are most often expressed in words, and those internal words impact how you see the world. In relationship terms your internal and spoken words create the business impression you give and relationships you have.

One of my favorite words to "pick on" is the word "but." I tell my clients to get rid of it. Period. No buts.

Why?

"But" is a modifying word that negates whatever came before it. It is contrary and takes exception to the first thing said. It implies the phrase after "but" is more important.

So, if I say, "I like my business, but getting customers is too hard." I have just made the "hard" more important than the "like". In fact, I have negated the good part.

This happens elsewhere in your business relationships. "I like you as my partner, but you didn't do what I asked," makes the lack more important than the like. "I want to work on building my business, but I'm too tired of it all," means you really don't want to work on the business because you are too tired.

You see? "But" is ruining all your moments of possible gain.

Instead, use "and", switch phrases, or don't add the negative to the statement at all. "I like my business," is much more positive. "I am really tired, and I still want to work on the business" gives a much better impression and hope for the future. "You didn't do what I asked, but I still like you as my partner" makes the positive most important.

Now, don't be sneaky and try to use other words for but. "However", "Although", and "Nevertheless" have the same impact. If you need to say both things keep the positivity going - switch the ideas and put "and" in there.

Why would you want to stay positive in your business? Positive attitude builds your business, negativity breaks it down. Positivity is the growth encouraging fertilizer for your business success.

Thoughtful Questions:

What negative words do you use regularly about your business?

_____

_____

_____

_____

What negative words or ideas do you think about your business?

_____

_____

_____

_____

How does "but" get in the way of doing well in your business?

_____

_____

_____

_____

How has being negative harmed your business, interactions with employees, or retention of customers?

_____

_____

_____

_____

Skillful Practice:

For two days pay attention to how often you say "but". Actually track it in the moment by putting check marks on a piece of paper. For the following day jot down what things you say "but" about and who you say it to. Look for patterns. For the last two days of that week catch yourself before you say "but" and decide how to change your statement into a more positive one.

As this is the last communication skill, I wish to remind you of the free checklist, "*Common Mistakes People Make in Communication.*" If you haven't already, go to eepurl.com/bU_Jdj right now to sign up for it!

Intrapersonal skills

Although communication skills are central to making your business take off, there are internal skills which, when you develop and practice them, make using the communication skills easier. These internal skills also keep you in a healthy place while growing your business to where you want it to be. They protect you, encourage you, and give you energy when things are tough. They are internal or intrapersonal skills.

In this section I will be touching on the following:

- The importance of keeping yourself centered – not too high, not too low, just right
- How to know what to share and how to appropriately contain yourself
- Determining your limits
- Understanding how your "self" comes into the business equation
- Developing trust through yourself

Skill #10 - Don't go one down

The first step in being an owner of a great business is to know, respect and care for yourself.

Do you really know yourself? Do you like and respect yourself?

I am talking about healthy self-esteem.

Healthy self-esteem comes from **inside**, it is the realization you have inherent worth just because you are alive. *You can neither lessen nor increase this worth*, it just is, and *this internal worth is the same as every other human being*.

It has nothing to do with belongings, behaviors, abilities, or what others think of you; it just is.

This step is one of the hardest that I walk my clients through. You have been taught for years that esteem comes from external sources. You are pushed to compete, to be better than others at things, to attain material things. The business you own, the car you drive, the house you have are all forms of **external esteem**.

These *external esteems do not change self-esteem*; it is internal.

There are multiple forms of external esteem. What others think about you is "other esteem". The things you can do such as parenting, athletics, proficiencies, and work are called "ability esteem". The knacks or talents you have are "skill esteem." Lastly, there is "behavior esteem" which has to do with your actions, what you have done or not done. These are all things you can esteem, but they are not self-esteem; they don't change your inherent worth.

"Wait!" I hear you cry, "Don't these things matter?"

To answer, let me present a metaphor: think of emergency medical technicians (EMTs). When EMTs come to the site of an accident on the road, they don't approach the victims and ask, "What do you do for work?" or "Are you nice to your employees?" or "Do others like you?" or "Are you skilled at math?" They look at each person as equal, and they triage for need only. They treat everyone as having the same inherent worth. That is the model for healthy self-esteem.

Think of self-esteem as the surface of the ground. You stand firmly on it and can move in any direction. It is solid and firm and it doesn't change. This horizontal line is where healthy self-esteem resides.

If you cannot stay on the ground with equal self-esteem, it will affect your business. Let me show you one problem with self-esteem and how it can negatively impact your business.

First, when you think of unhealthy self-esteem, aside from the "other esteems" I mentioned, what comes to mind? For most people in my office or presentations low self-esteem pops first into their mind.

What is low self-esteem? It is putting yourself down. It is telling yourself you are somehow less than, worth less, or one down from others or a particular person. It is an attack on that inherent worth called self-esteem.

The definition of healthy self-esteem is "the ability to hold yourself in appropriately warm positive regard despite your very human failings and very human successes." It means you realize you have worth no matter what. Low self-esteem negates this.

How could this impact your business? Here are a few ways:

- You tell yourself you aren't good enough and thus don't go after a business loan that could help grow your business

(mind you, it isn't about evaluating your business and seeing if it is able to get the loan, it is about personally feeling unworthy.)

- You may feel inferior to a competitor and thus not put in bids where she is because you "know" you'll "never get it."

- You may not approach certain possible customers because you feel you are less than them in some way (education, looks, connections, money.)

- You shut down in meetings because you tell yourself your ideas "don't matter" or "aren't as good as the other peoples'." Your ideas may be the tipping point that could help your business jump to the next level of the stratosphere, but because you stay quiet the business loses out.

In order to pull yourself out of this low self-esteem you need to recognize it. It usually shows up in negative self-talk with lots of "can't"s and "not enough"s. It also can be a physical sensation that is very draining; your body feels like it is melting or seeping away into the ground heavily. (This drain can negatively impact your business by undermining motivation and inspiration.)

When you catch these things say to yourself "I am enough and I matter even if...."

"I am enough and I matter, even if I'm not as educated as the person I'm speaking to." "I am enough and I matter even if my last business failed." "I am enough and I matter even if an employee just quit." "I am enough and I matter even if I didn't get that bid." "I am enough and I matter even if my ideas seem simple to me." (By the way, your "simple" ideas may be "revolutionary" to someone else. If you don't share them, there is no way to possibly move forward on them.)

Let me give you an example. Years ago I was in a training led by Terry Real, a nationally known relationship therapist. Participants were in small groups practicing new skills and as I was practicing doing the skill, Terry drifted over to observe our group. I immediately went into "I'm not good enough and I'm going to mess up!" Having just recently learned the mantra (in that training) I said to myself "I'm enough and I matter even if I mess up in front of Terry." It helped me center myself and speak realistically to myself. "Hey, he's been doing this for 30 years, and I just started learning it 3 months ago!" I was able to focus on the work and learning rather than my discomfort. Even when I did make a mistake in front of Terry I was able to hear his helpful feedback rather than shutting down in shame.

You see what the mantra does? It reminds you everyone stands on *equal* footing. My mother used to say to me "Kim, there will always be smarter and less intelligent people, prettier and less attractive, better than you or worse than you in something." She was encouraging me to realize everyone had strengths and weaknesses, or in other words, we all have our rows to hoe. It's picking up the hoe and getting to work without lingering in low self-esteem that moves us and our businesses forward.

Thoughtful Questions:

What things about yourself are you harsh about?

_____

_____

_____

_____

How do you slip into putting yourself down? How does it feel in your body?

_____

_____

_____

_____

What usually triggers it and what do you say to yourself?

_____

_____

_____

_____

When you go into that low place, how does it impact your business?

_____

_____

_____

_____

How long does it usually take for you to pull yourself out of it?

_____

_____

_____

_____

Skillful Practice:

For the next three days pay attention to yourself and identify when you go one down. Observe what things (events, thoughts, people) trigger these times of low self-esteem. Note in your journal how it impacts your mood, motivation, interactions, and business progress. You may also pay attention to people around you for indications of low self-esteem. For the rest of the week, any time you notice yourself going one down use the mantra "I'm enough and I matter" to center yourself and move forward. Take notes in your journal (or below) about your struggles and successes.

Skill #11 - Don't go one up

Going into a "less than" spot is not the only form of unhealthy self-esteem that can trip you up. Consider for a moment the social messages we get about emotional and relational health. Be independent, don't feel anything unless you choose it, be able to do everything for yourself, do not ask for help, feel better than others – society views that as health, as the ideal. It means being in charge of everything, on top of the world, more than other people.

Do you disagree?

The message is this type of "strength" is to be reached for. In other words, society views being "one up" as healthy.

Unfortunately, in all relationships, even business ones, being better than others is just as unhealthy as being needy, helpless, dependent, and feeling less than or "one down."

The middle ground is the healthy spot.

Lamentably we get the wrong message from the world. Competition and admiring your business skills is healthy, but only if viewed correctly.

Let me share an example. I had a client who was of genius level intelligence. He was smart, very physically able, and personable. When we started discussing self-esteem, he said "I have good self-esteem; I know I'm better than almost everyone at everything." While this statement may have been true, he still had unhealthy self-esteem. He wasn't a better person, he was just better at doing many things than others. He was going one up, and you can bet others in his life felt the attitude (it's the reason he was in my office.)

What does this have to do with your business?

By acting "better than" you lose touch with how your actions are affecting others around you, creating problems. Because you feel "better than" you act as if only you matter; not relational at all to your business associates. You act entitled. Being one up feels good; you don't have discomfort to encourage you to change (as happens in one down positions.) You have only the problems in your business – employees that leave because you lord over them, customers who feel talked down to and go to your competitors, vendors who go elsewhere, legal problems, and the list goes on. Being one up is much like being under the influence- you are judgment impaired.

Remember, we all have the same worth.

Being one up may feel good to you - it feels bad to the people around you. When you are in a better-than state you give an attitude which turns others off. (Remember Barry?) That's because being in the one-up position involves feeling contempt for others. When you feel this contempt, even a little, you no longer connect, and great business comes from great connections.

One insidious form of this contempt for others is distain for their choices – "I would NEVER do THAT!" This is called self-righteous indignation, and it is encouraged by society (back to cultural expectation that you be "better than" others.) Unfortunately, this is damaging to relationships in business. Because you judge the other person you are often not able to help them improve, really see them for who they are, and make a sale to them or work well with them.

How do you stop the damage? Simple, get humble. Easier said than done when you are feeling great in your one up position. Being humble means recognizing and embracing our common humanity. The mantra you say to yourself is "But for grace, there go I" or another way to conceptualize it is "I could make the same type of mistake myself."

It goes back to the lesson from my Mom - there will always be people better than you at things or not as good as you. Someone who has a skill you lack could be tempted to look down on you as not worthy, but that's not the truth of the matter. The truth is we all stand equal in worth. Skills, talents, looks, money, behaviors, business acumen, experience, connections, and all the "other" esteems do not change the fact we all stand on the same ground, equal in inherent worth.

So, when you are tempted to put yourself on a pedestal for all those "other" things, remember in each of those categories there will be better and worse off people. Not only are you enough and you matter, you are also capable of the same mistakes or failings as every other human being. By staying humble you make better decisions and make better connections with others in the business world.

[One final note about "other" esteems. It is perfectly normal to be proud of those things. It is not healthy or relational to think they make you *better* than other people. For example, Serena Williams can probably beat me at tennis with both hands tied behind her back. She can esteem her skill, talent and learning in tennis - that doesn't make her a better person than me. As people we stand inherently equal. As a tennis players she's leagues ahead of me and can be proud of that.]

Thoughtful Questions:

What "other" esteems trip you up? Which ones do you think are important? Are they more important to you than inherent worth? Why or why not?

_____

_____

Where did you learn to esteem these other things?

_____

_____

_____

_____

What would happen to you if all those other things you esteem
disappeared tomorrow?

_____

_____

_____

_____

How do you act when you are feeling better-than another person?

_____

_____

_____

_____

How could these behaviors negatively impact your business?

_____

_____

_____

_____

Have you ever interacted with someone who is in the one-up position? What was that like?

_____

_____

_____

_____

Skillful Practice:

For the next three days pay attention to yourself and identify when you go one-up. Observe what things (events, thoughts, people) trigger these times of entitled/overblown self-esteem. Note in your journal how it impacts your mood, behaviors, and business interactions. You may also pay attention to people around you for indications of one-up esteem. For the rest of the week, any time you notice yourself going one-up get humble and use the mantra "But for grace, there go I" to center yourself and move forward. Take notes in your journal (or below) about your struggles and successes.

Skill #12 - Do It "Just Right"

In the first section I taught you how to listen and then how to speak; however, do you know "what" to speak? How do you determine what things you can and should say to have healthy and successful business interactions?

You ask yourself three questions:

1. Is it true?
2. Is it considerate?
3. Is it necessary?

These questions will determine *what* you share with others in business. As a balance they keep you from overwhelming those around you or avoiding sharing what you need to share. If the answer isn't "Yes" to all of them, you don't share.

Let's explore each of them a little further.

1. Is it true?

When you ask yourself "Is it true" you are not only looking at the factual information about something, but you also are checking with yourself. Do you believe the information is true as well?

If you are not truthful with your business contacts, it will ultimately bite you in a tender spot. You might get away with it for a time, but at some future date it will catch up to you. Don't tell your boss you are deliriously happy with your job when you are miserable (we'll talk later about what you *can* say that is likely to get improvement and not lose your job.) Do not tell a coworker you are going to do a task if you aren't. Don't tell an employee "Everything is okay" when the business is struggling. Don't share research studies you don't believe in with your customer just to make a sale.

Here's a pretty solid rule for sales - if you are questioning your product, you really shouldn't be selling it in the first place. You will NOT be convincing if you fake belief. Red flags will be going off with everyone you try to pitch. It is important you believe in your product/service so you can help others see the value in it.

Lastly, about truth – it is important to realize the person you are sharing with will have their own truth. They may not believe what you say about your product or service. They may not agree with you about your dissatisfaction with the job. That is a fact of life and relationships; we don't always believe the same things as each other. This chapter is about sharing appropriately in a work setting; you only share about yourself, you don't control other people's truths.

2. Is it considerate?

This question confuses people in the work setting because they think it means you sugar-coat information. In no way do I mean that being considerate should rob information of its impact and importance (which is what sugar-coating often does.) Consideration in this question means using tact, diplomacy, and timing.

What you are really asking is "Do my words, attitude and timing help the other person hear and understand me?" I think "Is it considerate" is easier to remember.

Here are a few things that go into being considerate:

- Timing – you need to share when the person has the time and ability to hear you. Don't approach an employee for an intense discussion of their performance just before they need to go into a big sales meeting. Don't catch your boss right as he/she is leaving to go to their child's ball game to ask for a raise. Don't call a customer and expect to talk to them while they are sitting down to dinner. (By the way, I usually ask my clients "Is this a good time to talk" right after I say who is calling.)

- Topic Choice – speak to the other person on their level of interest and understanding. You wouldn't talk to a 5 year old about the universal string theory of gravity, don't talk with your customer about the specifics of research into your product unless it is something in which they have expressed interest. And, if they have asked about it, start very simply; as they ask more questions you may choose to increase complexity depending on their understanding. To make sure you are staying in their zone say, "Please, if you don't understand something I say, don't just nod your head. Ask me to repeat or explain further."

- Words Used – speak to people on their level and with their type of vocabulary. I love to read and have a pretty extensive vocabulary; however, I have to be careful when using it. Sometimes I have used a word and had a client ask, "What does that word mean?" When choosing your vocabulary, be aware of what your audience may or may not know, but don't assume. It is difficult because you don't want to be seen as talking down to someone by being too simplistic or too complex. I suggest you keep it informative, direct, and not flowery (unless you are poet, writer, or some other similar professional and they are expecting that type of language.) This leads to the next tip.

- Know your audience – speak to people as they would speak and expect to be spoken to. If you are a coach speaking in front of a church audience, you are pretty unlikely to swear; however, if you are with friends who swear, you might too. You have to choose how you want to interact and be viewed. However, swearing aside, if you are in a relaxed atmosphere with a business contact, and you remain rigid and professionally stuck-up, it will create tension. If you have a superior, colleague or client who appreciates "straight shooting" you do well to come to the point.

- Avoid jargon – Catch phrases and jargon abound in all areas of life and especially in business. Avoid using jargon especially when speaking to clients. This means you should also avoid acronyms. Of course, if you are giving a professional presentation to an audience who understands the jargon (know your audience) you can sprinkle acronyms and jargon in, but always identify what they mean the first time you use them. There is nothing worse than being in a meeting and not knowing what the speakers are "babbling" about. I highly suggest you avoid catch-phrases and overused phrases.It may be a big paradigm shift for you to think outside the box, but critical thinking will get you ahead. (Did you see what I did there?)

3. Is it necessary?

When you are asking this question you are seeing if you should share it and if you need to share it. Necessity resides on a continuum.

   SHOULD it be said? (over-sharing).... to.... Does it NEED to be said? (under-sharing)

We all know a person who has no filter between their brain and their mouth. They live on the left side of this line. Everything they think comes out whether or not it is necessary. In business this is the sales person who "sells past the sale" or the employee who always has comments about what is going on around them. It is too much and not necessary.

On the other end of the continuum is the question of "need". Some things do need to be said, and there are people who struggle to say things even if they are needed. Earlier I shared the importance of making requests. This is one area where businesses that don't cultivate relationships correctly miss out. They don't ask for the sale or give their customers some way to help them. Those are discussions that **need** to happen.

Another place necessary comes into play is in being direct to employees or vendors. You must ask yourself if the thing you are going to bring up needs to be said. I hear people say "I pick my battles", then they never stand up for any battle, and ultimately they lose (money, customers, good employees, etc.) because they didn't speak when it was necessary.

True, considerate, and necessary are the guidelines for you to follow to "get it right" when speaking. They are seeds that will mature and bear great business fruit.

Thoughtful Questions:

Have you ever experienced a person who didn't believe in what they were selling or doing? What was it like to interact with them? What feeling did you take away about the product or service?

_____

_____

_____

_____

Have you ever tried to sell or profit from something you didn't believe in? What was that like? How successful were you? Did you stick with it or leave?

_____

_____

_____

_____

How are you at taking into account the fact that people each have their own truth? How might that impact your business?

_____

_____

_____

_____

In what ways do you fall short when trying to speak to another person in a kind manner?

_____

_____

_____

_____

Which of the things listed (timing, topic, words, audience, jargon) are you good at? Which do you need to work on?

_____

_____

_____

_____

Which end of the necessary spectrum do you spend the most time in? (over-sharing or under-sharing)

_____

_____

_____

_____

What makes you over- or under-share?

_____

_____

_____

_____

How do you think the struggles you have with true/kind/necessary
have impacted you in business?

_____

_____

_____

_____

Skillful Practice:

For the next two days take some notes on how you share and how
you currently decide to share. Notice when you feel pressure to
share or close down. Note any issues with timing, jargon, word
usage, missing your audience, and topic choices. Then, armed
with the insight you have gained, begin to ask yourself the three
questions before you share. Check in with yourself before sharing.
Journal about your experiences and what you learned.

Skill #13- Understand Your Limits

One mistake many people in business make is forgetting to understand and work with their limits. When you don't have limits, then there is nothing to push and nothing to strive for. There is also nothing to keep yourself and your business safe while it ripens and matures.

The basis of all business bounds are your personal limits. If your work does not reflect an understanding of these boundaries, then you will find yourself failing more than succeeding.

Personal limits include:

- How much time you have to give to business – this will vary over time
- What your business abilities are – you may need training or to hire others to shore up your weaknesses
- What you like or do not like to do – again, you may have to do things you don't like, and you may choose to hire people to do those things
- How you do or do not prefer to act – hopefully you will not act in ways that you find distasteful just to build your business
- What brings you a personal as well as professional return on investment – what are the ultimate benefits for being in and doing the business you do?
- The give-and-take between your business and personal life – do they foster or fight each other?

Your business also should have limits. They will determine the how, what, and who of your business and/or where you work.

Business limits include:

- What the business is good at. Your business can't be good at everything. When I worked at a bank for a summer job, we were encouraged to ask customers if they would like us to save them time or money. We were selling products, but it showed what the bank was trying to be good at, saving time or money for their customers. They weren't trying to sell the prettiest checks. You should ask yourself what the business is good at, what need is it filling, and how is it filling it?
- The legal limits on the business. What can and can't you do legally?
- What does the business (or you) want to do? Take a look at the goals of the business and consider if they are in alignment with the personal limits you have discovered.
- What the business is able to do. This means looking at the training and capabilities of the business. It means taking into consideration how big the business is and how much work it can take on. It also means reviewing what the business wants to do; taking on something you "can" do but don't "want" to do is a recipe for disaster.
- How and how fast the business is growing (and is capable of growing.)
- What people the business works with. You are creating an overall business culture, so make sure the people who come into contact with that culture support it. This is about the type of business your business does work with. Do you have limits such as only wanting to work with Green businesses? It also means looking at your vendors, customers, partners, and employees. An example of one limit in my business is the expectation of respect. Disrespectful people and businesses are respectfully disconnected from.

To determine your personal, professional, and business limits, you must comprehend and appreciate your values. Your values flow throughout your personal and professional life. If either your personal or professional life do not match your values, you will be wasting a ton of energy and drive that would help you take off. These values are core and become important to you, your business, and all the people who work with your business. They are often the reason other professionals and customers choose to work with you.

I'd like to suggest you purchase Mike Michalowitz's book "The Pumpkin Plan" to really dig down into your values and limits. He has a great process to determine your values and then create what he calls "Immutable Laws" for your business. (The rest of the book is really good too!) For example, the laws for my business, Creating Rewarding Relationships, are: 1. Enjoyable learning is lifelong learning, 2. R-E-S-P-E-C-T (sing it!), 3. Anti-Drama, and 4. Love is a Verb. These four ideas and ideals guide my business every day. I'm hoping you are experiencing #1 in this book!

Thoughtful Questions:

What were the messages you learned growing up about values and business?

_____

_____

_____

_____

What values do you currently hold about work and business?

_____

_____

_____

_____

What do you consider of primary importance in work and business?

_____

_____

_____

_____

What business attitudes do you want to cultivate in yourself and others?

_____

_____

_____

_____

What attitudes or behaviors will you not accept in yourself or your business?

_____

_____

_____

_____

Who have you respected in business? (Someone you know or someone you know about.)

_____

_____

_____

_____

What do you think their values and limits were around their business? Their life?

_____

_____

_____

_____

Skillful Practice:

Read a biography (preferably an autobiography) about someone you highly respect and want to have a similar business or life attitude like. Do not base your choice solely on business success or money; instead consider what that person's life and attitudes were. While reading identify what limits and laws they followed in their life and business. If you are curious, get Mike's book "The Pumpkin Plan" and read it. You will determine many of your own values and how they relate to your business life.

Skill #14 - HALT

People often fail to recognize an important fact in business exchanges - how you feel affects your reactions. This is true in all aspects of your life.

If you are feeling tired, irritated, hurt, or depressed, your reactions are unlikely to be positive. You come to work exhausted from a rough night with your child, and a customer asks a tough question- you snap, get grumpy, and short. Or you may shut down, shut them out, and "run away." None of these responses are helpful or likely to connect you with your customer.

HALT yourself.

Both responses (lashing out or shutting down) could be due to the way you were feeling when you walked into work- not the actual question your customer (employee, business partner, vendor, etc.) asked.

Be aware of HALT. The letters stand for **H**ungry, **A**ngry, **L**onely, and **T**ired. These are triggers for poor business responses.

When you are hungry your blood sugar is often low. Lowered blood sugar can result in poor concentration, poor decision making, and sluggish responses. Hunger also increases irritability. None of these help your business.

When you are angry, your reactions are often exaggerated. Your emotional response can be extreme. You may make decisions and say things you later regret. Anger often triggers the stress response which makes it difficult to see alternatives, be open to new ideas, empathize with others, and make thoughtful rather than reactive decisions. Any of these anger induced reactions can damage your business.

Loneliness is one of the most difficult emotions for people to express or own up to; however, it can have a big impact on your reactions and business. If you are feeling lonely, you are less likely to reach out for help when you or your business needs it. Loneliness even makes you perceive your stress as worse than someone who has the exact same stressor but feels linked to others. Feeling connected creates motivation and drive to meet life and business challenges; when you don't feel that way you lose those things and it impacts your business.

Lastly, tiredness can be a major problem. Recent studies have shown that Americans (and many people in other Western countries) are chronically sleep deprived. For some reason, we have taken on an idea that sleep is a waste of time rather than a real physical and psychological need. When you are tired you have inferior judgment. Poor sleep worsens memory, hampers learning, impacts mood and motivation, and can lead to injuries and accidents on the job. It leads to lost productivity, errors, reduced efficiency, and lack of critical thinking. I would hope you want none of these effects in your business.

Take a few moments to HALT yourself and make sure your business is not halted.

Thoughtful Questions:

What emotions trip you up the most?

_____

_____

_____

_____

How do you act when you are in each of the HALT situations?

_____

_____

_____

_____

How can you identify for yourself what emotion you are feeling **before** you react badly to a situation that has nothing to do with the emotion?

_____

_____

_____

_____

How good are you at identifying your emotions? Can you describe each of your emotions to yourself and others?

_____

_____

_____

_____

Skillful Practice:

Whether you are feeling out of contact in your business or you are just out of balance from something else, take a moment to register where you are at *before* you respond. Take a deep breath and ask yourself "How am I feeling? How is that feeling about this situation and how much is about something else?" If your current mood precludes healthy reactions, then take a step back. Ask to talk when you are feeling less of the HALT.

Added practice: email me to get a list of emotion words and take time to think about how each of those emotions impacts you and your business. Practice appropriately describing and expressing them. (Kim@CreatingRewardingRelationships.com)

Skill #15 - PMA

About 7 years ago my husband and I rescued a puppy, a Papillion. At the time he was about 3.5 pounds, and my husband chose to name him Thor. That's right, Thor, the god of thunder!

The name gets real chuckles out of anyone who hears it the first time while meeting the now 6.5 pound dog. But you know what? It fits. Aside from the ears which look like Thor's winged helmet- I swear our Thor swings a hammer of cuteness which fells even the grumpiest of arch enemies.

It's all in how he approaches them. He is overjoyed to see each and every person or dog who comes into his field of view. Thor exudes excitement and transmits it through his quivering hairs, pricked ears, and joyous grin. He has positive mental attitude (PMA). It is contagious, and people smile back, ask to pet him, and make of him.

So, why is this important for a business book?

How you are treated and how people respond to you has a lot to do with how you approach people.

If you approach with a scowl, your employee will be put on guard against you. If you look blank or act distracted, your business partner may not pay attention to you either. If you smile and are warm, your business contacts will be more open to you. PMA works.

It's not hard, but how often do you forget it?

How often do you:
- Growl at your employee before giving them feedback?
- Make the effort to smile while talking on the phone?
- Greet your partner with a hearty hello when you see them?

- Make a request with a scowl?
- Remember this person matters before you talk about something difficult?
- Express your respect non-verbally as well as verbally?

You see I have no doubt Thor loves me. He grins at me as he runs to me on our walks. He watches my face when I talk to him. He dances at the door when I come home. He loves to curl in my lap with his favorite chew toy. He shows me he cares and thinks I'm important. His PMA says more than any words could express.

Do you do that for the people you work with? Can you imagine how customers would react to you if you always helped them feel important? If you do, good for you, keep it up! If not, think of ways you can show and speak your respect and excitement.

Take a tip from Thor, smile often; it helps you connect and grow that business.

Thoughtful Questions:

In what areas of your business are you most likely to be negative? Why?

_____

_____

_____

_____

How can you change your attitude about those areas?

_____

_____

_____

_____

How do you think a change in your negative approach would impact those areas?

_____

_____

_____

_____

How has negativity impacted your business?

_____

_____

_____

_____

How has being welcoming, happy, and smiling helped your business?

_____

_____

_____

_____

How can you better convey pleasantness, respect, and gratitude in all areas of your business?

_____

_____

_____

_____

Skillful Practice:

Identify one area (or person) in your business where you find yourself being negative. Brainstorm ways to be more positive in this area or to this person. Practice those positive behaviors for a week and keep track in your journal. Track your reactions, struggles, mood, and successes. Jot down the changes you perceive in your business or yourself due to that attitude change.

Skill #16 - Mindful Representation

The other day I was rather rudely (and dangerously) cut off in traffic by a work truck. Plastered all over the side, back, and windows of this truck was the name of the remodeling company. Want to bet who I won't ever be calling? Want to bet which company will have a bad taste associated with it for a long time if not forever? Want to bet what company I'll steer others away from? I may not remember this particular incident, but I'll remember I don't like them much for some reason.

Before you argue driving ability has nothing to do with their ability in remodeling, keep this in mind – they were "on." That person was driving a rolling billboard, but forgot. I mean, they were representing their company in all they do - including their driving. The message it gives me is I can't trust them to be careful with my remodeling work if they are careless with their driving. I can't think they'll be polite to me in person if they are rude to me on the road.

So, what does this have to do with your business? Simple, you are "on" at all times; you are a walking billboard for who you and your business are.

If you are mean and rude to your employees, what will your customer think about you? If you nag and are negative to your spouse on the phone, what impression are you giving your employees? If you talk mean about or belittle others around the water cooler, how will a colleague feel when talking to you? Will he worry you are talking down about him to others? If you talk about how you "screw" your competitors or customers, will your business partners think you are trustworthy?

This isn't about how you treat people "in the moment"; it is about how you treat your life and those around you all the time. You represent yourself every minute of your life, not just at work – your business acquaintances see and take away impressions on everything you do.

You can say "it's not fair, I'm nice to my colleagues," but if you are nasty elsewhere you'll give your associates something to worry about. You can say "I'd never do that to them," but they now know you are capable of such things, which means you are capable of doing it to them.

Consider your life and business relationships as interconnected rather than separate. There are consequences to everything you do (positive or negative.) Your actions, words, and attitude all cause impressions – think carefully what impression you want to leave and act accordingly.

Thoughtful Questions:

How have you been talking about others at work or in your business?

_____

_____

_____

_____

How do you treat people who aren't central to your business while at work?

_____

_____

_____

_____

What impression do you give personal contacts about you as a business person? How do you think they feel about referring to you, utilizing your services, or working with you?

_____

_____

_____

_____

If you drive a vehicle that represents your company, what impression do you think your driving gives to potential customers, vendors and business associates?

_____

_____

_____

_____

Do you gossip, pass stories, or gather rumors? How do you think this affects your interactions in your business?

_____

_____

_____

_____

Skillful Practice:

Take out your journal and turn to a blank page. In the center write "Representation" and circle it. Set a timer for ten minutes and brainstorm every word, phrase, or idea that comes to mind about how you represent your business in your life. Look at all areas of your life – e.g. on the job, at home, in public, with friends, with colleagues, at worship, at your kid's school, you name it. As the idea comes up, put a line out from the circle and write the word. If another idea related to that one comes up, add it to the first line with a second line. Each new individual idea gets its own radial line. At the end of ten minutes look at your mind map and jot down your thoughts. Afterward, ask yourself how you could improve your representation of your business daily.

Skill #17 - Turn up the Trust

Trust in business (and life) is like a dimmer switch; it isn't just on or off.

Trust is not something you are "given"; it is something you earn. You earn trust at the beginning of a new business relationship (with a customer, an employee, a partner, an investor). You also sometimes need to earn trust again after a mistake has been made. Occasionally you may have to work to earn trust because someone else broke a person's trust (like a customer who was "burned by the last guy.")

When you are new to a person or potential customer, they are not going to immediately trust you. With a dimmer switch you slowly turn on the light; that's how trust comes into being - slowly. You build all trust a little at a time through your words and your actions.

How do you earn trust?

You are trustworthy; you do trustworthy things, and you are stable and dependable. As you do this, the light gets brighter- the person trusts you more, the switch is turned up. Any time you do something that makes the business associate question your reliability, you lose ground on trust; the light dims. Depending on how big the breach of trust is, the light may click off; you'll have to work doubly hard to get it to even start coming on.

It is a slow process, but it is real, and you have control over it. You make the choice to act in a trustworthy fashion.

In business being trustworthy means:

- Doing what you said you would.
- Completing things in the timeframe you said you would.

- Holding to commitments.
- Being up front if something changes. In other words, communicate with everyone impacted by the change, from worker to customer.
- Owning up to mistakes as soon as possible and work to "make good" on them. [By the way, one way to kill trust is to ruin an apology with an excuse.]
- Being clear in what you are looking for in your business contacts. This includes creating a great customer (see earlier chapter), telling your employees exactly what is expected of them, and keeping partners or investors up to date on what is needed for the business.
- Being honest about money matters.
- Not agreeing to something you aren't willing or able to do.
- Not lying.
- Reaching out to help your business associates, and if you offer to help, follow through.
- Making sure your employees and other business representatives follow the same honesty and trust expectations.
- Referring your customers and colleagues to other great professionals.

By building a trusting relationship with customers, employees, partners, and investors, you make them all a part of your business. When they trust you and your business they invest in it with their time, emotions, and money. That sort of investment makes your business take off.

Thoughtful Questions:

In what ways have you seen trust broken in your industry?

_____

_____

_____

_____

In what ways have you disappointed or broken the trust of a
business associate?

_____

_____

_____

_____

When has your trust been broken in business? Were you able to
re-trust that person or business? What needed to happen for you
to trust again?

_____

_____

_____

_____

When something goes wrong for a customer, what policies and
procedures do you have in place to make sure you make every
effort to keep the trust of that person?

_____

_____

_____

_____

Skillful Practice:

Every time you decide to do something in your business, ask yourself, "is this a trustworthy action?" Think to yourself "*I make trust the old fashioned way; I earn it.*" Filter each decision and action, and be *honest*– will it look trustworthy from ALL angles? If you have to defend it in any way, it is probably not. Journal about what you learn.

Interpersonal Skills – Getting Along with Others

In your business it is a given you will come into contact with people who are difficult or unlikeable. When you have strong interpersonal skills, you not only relate well with those you like, but you can also deal with those that "push your buttons." Margaret Mead said it best when she said, "I have a respect for manners as such; they are a way of dealing with people you don't agree with or like."

In this section you will learn:

- Why manners matter
- When and how to say "no" such that it helps your business
- The power of silence
- Conflict 101
- How to be on the "A" list
- The importance of Truth, Respect, and knowing when to multitask

These interpersonal skills are the fertilizer to make your business to shoot up toward the sky. Let's get started.

Skill #18 - Say Please

One of the most basic manners we learn at an early age is to say "please." That single word smoothes the way, sets a positive tone, and creates an atmosphere of cooperation rather than coercion. It also opens opportunities to grow your business organically and swiftly.

"Please" is associated with charm and appeal. It makes what you are asking more attractive. It becomes no longer a demand but a request, which people are more likely to agree to do. If you consistently use please appropriately, you create preference toward you and your business. It is linked to the word "oblige" or "accommodate" which means your customer, vendor, or employee becomes more willing to find ways to help you.

[A tangent on helping. People love to help; it makes them feel good. Studies have shown small acts of helping like holding a door for someone decreased the stress response in people and boosted their daily well-being. Additionally, more helping behaviors meant more positive feelings and more robust mental health. Therefore, when you say "Please help me" you are giving your customer, vendor, or employee a chance to have better health.]

You use "please" to build trust and especially when you make requests (see earlier chapters on trust and requests.) Aside from creating willingness in the listener, "please" acknowledges you are making a request. You are asking for something from the other person, and please lets them know you are aware they don't have to do what you are asking.

Using "please" does not make you weak. By saying "please" you give the message you are strong enough to make a request and to recognize the other person in the interaction. You are showing respect which is never a weakness.

There are some times when "please" should be avoided, and many of them are in the written word. Unfortunately, many "please" phrases have become outmoded and a bit stiff. "Please don't hesitate to contact" can better be said "Please contact me." "Please be advised" is often misused to say "I'm giving you information" rather than in the correct context of "I'm giving you advice." Lastly, when you tack "please" onto the end of a sentence, written or spoken, it can easily be misconstrued. It is often seen as coercive, sarcastic, or ominous. If you are using "please", put it toward the beginning of your sentence.

"Please" is a smoother-of-the-way; it is a big part of the grease which helps civilization, companies, and organizations function despite disparate personalities, needs, and wants. In business, "please" allows you to make appropriate requests which help your business take off.

Thoughtful Questions:

In what situations (or with what people) do you struggle to use the word "please"?

_____

_____

_____

_____

What are the messages you learned in your life about the word "please"?

_____

_____

_____

_____

How do you respond to "please"?

_____

_____

_____

_____

Can you think of any situations you have experienced where you think "please" might have helped?

_____

_____

_____

_____

When have you seen "please" misused? (e.g. sarcastically, with a poor attitude, etc.)

_____

_____

_____

_____

Skillful Practice:

For the next week, pay attention to when the word "please" is used by yourself or other people. Take note of how it is used and how it is responded to. Is it used in an attitude of request, or with a tone or inflection that dismisses the person being asked? Record in your journal any phrases with "please" in them that you like. At the end of the week start using "please" in all of your requests. When I say all of your requests I mean every single one; for example, when I ask the guy to pump my gas I say "please" or when I order my drink at a restaurant I say it. Get into the habit of "please" as a natural extension of every request.

Skill #19 - Just Say Thank You

As great as it feels to be recognized in our business, many people feel uncomfortable and struggle to accept compliments with aplomb. Two simple words can work wonders in this situation.

Just say "Thank you."

Seems easy, right? Yet, business people mess it up all the time.

How? They add things! When they add, they end up negating the compliment. Here are the types of things people say after "Thank you":

- "Anyone could have done it." (Usually not anyone could have done it, and even if they could have, they didn't, you did!)
- "It was no big thing." (You insulted the compliment giver by telling them what they thought was important really wasn't.)
- "I had to do it." (What does this matter? You still did it, ultimately chose to do it, and the person is appreciating it.)
- "It was a team effort." (Most likely the person knows it is a team effort, and even if they didn't, they are still complimenting you at this moment. This holds especially true for projects where you were the leader – recognize your contributions)
- Point out the problems or faults in the thing you are being complimented for. (By doing this you are telling the compliment giver they are too dense to have noticed what was wrong. You are insulting them.)

Ultimately, with statements like above you are rude to the person who gave you the compliment. You are implying they somehow don't know what they are talking about and are wrong in their compliment. Do you want to do that in your business?

Here's an easy way to stick to this skill; say "Thank you" and then close your mouth. If you are struggling inside to accept it, imagine you are saying "Thank you for taking the time and thought to compliment me." I am not encouraging you to say "Thank you. Yes, I'm the best ever." I'm suggesting you be kind and realize "thank you" is necessary.

Why is it necessary to be able to accept compliments? Because compliments are one way your business takes off. In networking meetings often people give testimonials about other professionals. If you can't accept them gracefully, then you undermine this important aspect of networking. When you are in meetings and someone gives you a compliment, it is a stepping stone to more business. Others note what you are good at and think of ways to capitalize on those skills. Your business begins to take off.

Bottom line, "Thank you" is about respect and good manners. It isn't about (or shouldn't look like) being egotistical. Take a breath, be cool, and stay pleasant. A matter of fact "thank you" is a return compliment of its own.

Thoughtful Questions:

Which of the statements above do you say after "thank you'?

_____

_____

_____

_____

How are you at accepting compliments? Do you brush them off? Do you get mad? Do you get embarrassed? Do you assume it is not an honest compliment? Do you think it is exaggerated? Do you ignore it and say nothing? Etc.

_____

_____

_____

_____

What assumptions do you have about compliments?

_____

_____

_____

_____

Do you seek out appropriate compliments? E.g. do you ask for testimonials, reviews, and recommendations?

_____

_____

_____

_____

Do you give compliments? How does it feel when people don't accept them? When they do?

_____

_____

_____

_____

Skillful Practice:

For one week simply say "thank you". Just accept the compliment
– don't argue, don't explain, don't negate. Think of the
compliment giver. Jot down your thoughts in your journal (or
below.)

Skill #20 - Ask the Big Question

Many people, when trying to build their business or work life, ask the wrong questions. They ask "How can I get ahead" or "How can I grow this part of my company" or "What do I need to do to _____ (succeed, solve my business shortcomings, etc.)." There is a bigger question truly successful business people have understood and used for years.

"How can I help you?"

Savvy business owners and managers ask this question of customers, vendors, employees, and themselves. They understand offering to help and then helping produces returns. Asking how you can help is a big deal.

Too often businesses leave customers feeling like they are the ones helping – "Buy our stuff so we can grow", "Come to our presentation" (so we have people there), and "Take our survey to let us know what you want" (to buy, to sign up for, to participate in.) Although sales and service should be about the customer, frequently it ends up being about … well, making sales.

When you ask the customer how you can help them, it sends a few messages. First, in asking them you allow them put forth some ideas. This tells them they are important in the process; in addition, it lets you gather useful information about what your business could be doing. Secondly, you acknowledge there is some sort of need or pain point the customer has. This can be greatly empowering to your customer who may have been told they are silly or don't need to worry about what they are trying to change. It may be a relief to them to have their needs recognized (if not fulfilled.) Lastly, you are implying that you CAN help them; letting them see you as the go-to for what they need. You want your customers to see you as the solution so they come to you and send others to you.

Don't forget once you have a customer to continue to ask how you can help them. They may need help understanding your product or service. They may need clarification on why the product or service is a good fit for them. You want them to use your product or service and enjoy it so they continue to be a customer and become an advocate.

Customers are not the only people you should be asking how you can help; you should be asking employees/consultants and vendors. When they feel heard and their needs are addressed as much as you can then you get the best work from them. You save time and money by asking this question rather than waiting for things to go wrong and make clear something isn't working. Their satisfaction is money in your business, ultimately.

Even employees can benefit from asking this question. If you aren't asking your superior what you can do to help them get what they want and where they want to go, then you don't have leverage to speak about where **you** are going.

Make no assumptions that you know what any of these business contacts need. They are not you; you have to ask. Ask them directly. Ask in an email. Send out a survey.

The underlying question you are really asking is "How can I help you give me more of what the business needs?" It isn't a manipulative question; it is about creating the best employees, customers, and vendors for your business. By helping them you help your business. You don't force them, you encourage them. Their participation then feels like a gift from them to you, and who doesn't like to give gifts?

Thoughtful Questions:

How do you currently get feedback from customers, employees and vendors?

_____

_____

_____

_____

Have you ever asked how you can help a business contact/associate in a meaningful way?

_____

_____

_____

_____

What concerns do you have about asking the big question?

_____

_____

_____

_____

What do you think about asking an employee or vendor how you can help them?

_____

_____

_____

_____

Has anyone ever asked you this question in your business or past business? If so, what was your experience and how did it impact you?

_____

_____

_____

_____

Skillful Practice:

One way to track the things your customers want help in is to track complaints. Look back at (or think back over) the complaints or problems your customers have had. What theme appears? What do you think the underlying need is that has been missed? Take some time to create questions you can ask your customers in order to hear what they want help with. Follow-up with current customers and ask them outright "What can I help you with today?" Do your best to help with what they ask for, even if it's not in your business. [I have created great referral systems by telling customers about other professional resources. You bet those customers think highly of me, come back to me for the services I provide, and refer others.]

Skill #21 - Know HOW to say No

Have you ever said "no"? Of course you have (especially when you were two!) Have you always used "no" responsibly? (I can see you looking quizzical.) Do you know what a responsible and irresponsible "no" are? They can be the difference between an average business and one that takes off.

"No" is a powerful word; it is a word meaning "stop", "enough", "here's my limit," and it is a great business word unless misused.

You probably know it is important to say "no" to things you don't want, like going to a meeting when you have a previous commitment, or giving your friend another "business loan" which will never be paid back. These are healthy times to use "no" as long as it is done respectfully.

However, in business this little word needs to be used with tact and responsibility or it becomes destructive.

For example, let's say a business contact wants to talk about something and you aren't ready. You have every right to say "no" to conversation at that time, but if you use the word to shut them down totally, you will ultimately lose out. Shutting someone down with "no" kills communication, connection, and space for business growth.

So, use "no" responsibly.

How do you do this? **A responsible no has three parts**: *the no, the reason, and an offer.* When your business associate asks if you can talk, and you aren't ready (let's say you just came out of an intense meeting) you can say,

1. "Not right now [*the no*]....
    - I'm still thinking about a meeting I was just in and need to write up some notes [*the reason*]....

- Could we talk this afternoon after lunch?" [*the offer*]

You have just used "no" responsibly. You have *not* shut your business associate down; you have honestly shared your need and recognized there is something the other person needs. You are also admitting now isn't a good time- respecting both yourself and your business associate. It is a good deal.

There are three "don'ts" to keep in mind when using a responsible "no".

1. Don't put off talking for more than 48hours. I prefer you talk the same day, but if you have to put it off longer [say it's right before work ends and you have another commitment] then schedule for the next day. That way you both will be likely to actually talk rather than let it go and become a business problem.
2. Don't constantly put a business contact off, they'll make up they are never of primary importance.
3. Don't use rescheduling as a way to gain time to "gather arguments." You'll only end up fighting rather than fixing problems.

If you are trying to say "no" to someone who wants to talk too often for your business, set a time once a week to talk and stick to it. "Hey, I know you want to talk. I am busy and can't do it right now, but we have tomorrow's weekly meeting. Please bring it up then."

Lastly, if you are saying "no" to the business mooch, you can still do so responsibly. Say, "No, I will not lend you money [the no] because you still owe me $500 from last summer [reason]. I suggest you look at other ways to get that money. I'd be willing to help you brainstorm ways you can do that. [offer]"

Respect yourself and your business associates enough to not shut communication down but open it up with your responsible use of "no".

Thoughtful Questions:

What do you think about saying "No"?

_____

_____

_____

_____

What messages have you learned over your lifetime about saying "No"? (e.g. from family, friends, peers, trainings, or business interactions.)

_____

_____

_____

_____

How do these messages impact how you do or don't use "No?"

_____

_____

_____

_____

What is your biggest struggle in using "No"?

_____

_____

_____

_____

What do you think your biggest hurdle will be in using a
responsible "No"?

_____

_____

_____

_____

Skillful Practice:

Think back through your business history and in your journal
make a list of the times "No" has impacted you or your business
life positively or negatively. Include times when "No" was used or
when you didn't say it but wished you had. Identify people
currently in your business life that you think you should use a
responsible "No" with. Over the next week take time to use a
responsible "No" with them and record how it goes. Jot down
what you learn and how you could improve.

Skill #22 - Know WHEN to say No

Now you know HOW to say "no" in your business; do you know WHEN to say it?

Keep in mind "no" makes room for "yes." If you are saying "yes" to every customer, whether or not they are right for you, there will come a time when you no longer have space for the best customers and you are left with "meh" customers. "No" creates space. It also gives you the chance to say "yes" to changes in your business. There may be things you are doing that no longer have a return on investment. It is time to say "No" to them so you can say "Yes" to the things that bring in money and customers. Additionally, saying "no" allows you to carve out the all-important time to say "Yes" to the rest of your life.

"No" is also important when the time isn't right in your business for "Yes." For example, the business needs time to stabilize from a major change. You need to hire staff. You or your staff doesn't have the training or expertise to take on the project. The partner asking to join has a different direction than you do. The change goes against your immutable laws. The customer isn't right. There aren't enough hours to get the new thing done. It isn't actually in your business purview. These are all times to say "no" for your business.

"No" can also save you from trouble. It keeps your reputation clean when you refuse to take on things you can't do. You want to deliver as promised, not overextend and then disappoint. You may also avoid legal problems associated with doing things you aren't trained or ready for. If you do over-extend it is because you have said "Yes" too often. Sometimes you may have to eat a little crow in order to get back on good footing. (Reread the section about apologies if you need a review.) It is better to have less to do, over-deliver and have happy employees/customers than to over-extend and make everyone unhappy. This smears your business reputation, and reputation is hard to regain.

Sometimes you need to say "No" because something no longer works for your business. Maybe your business changed since you first started working with a particular vendor and they are no longer a good fit. Maybe the customer, employee, or vendor changed and you are not a good fit for them. Maybe the services or product you offer didn't work for them despite all your best efforts. If you respectfully identify that lack of fit and encourage the business associate in their search for another connection, they will be left with a positive impression of your business.

Lastly, you may use "No" when something just "doesn't feel right." As much as we use cognition in business, our professional gut often gives us great feedback. If you have to force a "Yes," then "No" is a better response. Maybe you need more time to gather information or think about the idea. Time and time again I have heard business owners say, "I knew it wasn't a good idea, but I pushed myself to do it and it bit me in the behind." If you find you need to convince yourself to a "Yes", step back, ask yourself why, and then say "No" until you find a way to be comfortable.

Thoughtful Questions:

When have you said "yes" but later wished you said "no"?

_____

_____

_____

_____

How has a "yes" that should have been a "no" impacted your business?

_____

_____

_____

_____

How do you keep an eye on return on investment in order to determine what to keep doing and what to change?

_____

_____

_____

_____

How do you determine your business is ready for a change?

_____

_____

_____

_____

How do you let go of vendors/customers/employees who are no longer a fit for your business? Do you have a policy to help with this?

_____

_____

_____

_____

What "yeses" could you take advantage of if you used "no" in your business more often?

_____

_____

_____

_____

Skillful Practice:

Take a look at your business as it is currently. Jot down at least three areas where you think the appropriate use of "no" would help. Identify three places you could say "yes" once you practice "no". Decide which of the areas you are going to start with, and use "no" in the next week. Record your experience and how you can improve. Keep practicing.

Skill #23 - Handle Conflict

Do you do whatever you can to avoid a fight?

Do you go out of your way to not bring up things that may upset others? What if those things are important to you and your business?

Do you "forget" to call a customer or vendor who may be upset with you?

Do you evade a question and act like it wasn't said to avoid a possible confrontation?

Do you not reply to an invitation or "forget" to go to an event?

If this describes you, you have a major problem. You are conflict avoidant, and that's unhealthy for you and your business.

Now, before you say, "Hey, it's not good to cause strife or pick a fight!" I want you to read on.

I agree being argumentative or aggressive is not good for business, but *so is being passive and avoidant*. It is worse than being a doormat; it is being elusive and irritating. It can kill your business.

How?

One thing avoiding conflict does is send the wrong message. When you duck and run you leave business contacts feeling unheard and unimportant. Your evasions send the message you don't think of others, only yourself.

In addition, no change or business improvement comes about through ignoring problems. Ostriches get the bony finger pointed at them as the poster children for heads in the sand, but if you habitually avoid conflict, you are worse than the flightless bird.

Problems only become bigger, or your business associates begin to distance from you, as you duck and weave.

Unfortunately, your evasions usually cause what you fear the most, a blowup!

Conflict is not a bad thing. It is how you handle conflict that can be the problem. The good news is you can learn to handle it in a healthy way.

My husband once shared a metaphorical story from a management training class.

"You are shipwrecked on a deserted island. In your broken boat you find a single tool, a hammer. So, for the next few weeks you use that hammer for everything- chopping down trees, prying open coconuts, and even hammering a few nails. Then one day you bump an unknown compartment in that little boat of yours and out falls a kit with screw drivers, pliers, utility knives – a full assortment of tools. Would you continue to use the hammer for everything? Would you use the screwdriver to pound those nails?"

Many people only know of one way to deal with conflict, but there are several ways and no one technique is right in every situation.

Here are a few examples of conflict styles, when they are good, and when you would be hammering nails with that screwdriver.

1. **Forcing**– *one* person has the *final say* and all the control. This is appropriate only if everyone has freely agreed to it or there is an authority figure whose position necessitates it (a boss or business owner.) It is appropriate if there is limited time ("Look, a fire, everyone out!") It is not good if there is a constant win-lose or people feel like their needs are ignored.

2. **Withdrawal**– You *avoid conflict* and give in while focusing on another's needs. This works when the topic really isn't important to you (like a business decision that doesn't impact your job.) However, it is inappropriate when it leads to resentment or poor self-esteem.

3. **Peacemaker**– You remain neutral at all costs. This has the same positives and negatives as the "Withdrawal" conflict style. However, peacemaking is not appropriate if you give up your control and input all the time.

4. **Assertive**– You are responsible only for your own behaviors and don't assume others will agree. You work toward a win-win without forcing. There are two main forms of assertive response to conflict. You may **compromise**– everyone gives something up to come to an agreement. This is inappropriate if the final solution is watered down and doesn't really address the original issue. You may also **collaborate**– everyone agrees who does what. Collaboration takes allot of time and is inappropriate if you need a quick answer.

As you can see, each of the conflict styles has a place in your business. You can't sit down and compromise in a burning building but can while making long range business plans. You agree to a level of forcing when you have a boss- remember Truman's famous desk quote, "The buck stops here"- the decision ends at the big wigs. It is okay to withdraw if you really don't care about a decision or outcome (as long as you don't give the impression you don't care about the business associate!) You can be a peacemaker as long as you still remain yourself and provide business input.

Handling conflict appropriately is a great skill to move your business into solid growth.

Thoughtful Questions:

What messages have you learned over your lifetime about conflict? (e.g. from family, friends, peers, trainings, and business interactions.)

_____

_____

_____

_____

How have you seen others handle conflict?

_____

_____

_____

_____

How do these messages and experiences impact how you do or don't handle conflict?

_____

_____

_____

_____

What is the policy in your business for handling conflict with customers?

_____

_____

_____

_____

What is the culture about conflict (or disagreement) in your business? What would you like it to be? How can you move it that way?

_____

_____

_____

_____

Skillful Practice:

Decide which of the conflict strategies you are deficient in. Determine which strategy is best in the situation you are in, and use it. Are you using your hammer when you could put a screwdriver to better use? Put that stratagem aside and chose the correct one. It is a choice.

Skill #24 - Multitask Tasks, not People!

If you are not giving your full attention to someone and instead doing other things while they are either in front of you or on the phone, you are multi-tasking them.

When you multi-task someone, they feel it. How do you feel when someone does that to you? Haven't you known when someone is listening to another person instead of you on the phone? Can you hear the hesitation in their answers and their distraction? What message are you giving to customers, vendors, and employees when you multitask them?

By multi-tasking you are missing out on **real** interaction and connection with the other person. You can't connect when you don't focus. Real focus grows your business.

Listening means paying attention to a person. It means you are trying to understand, empathize and be able to respond appropriately. You can't listen if you are distracted, and believe me, multitasking results in distraction.

A few years ago the world lost a wonderful elderly man who taught me the importance of interpersonal focus. Whenever I spoke with Father Vincent **he was totally present** with me. No one and nothing else existed for him as we talked. That regard was like the sun and rain for a flower – I was cherished and nurtured. I will miss it, and I when I share that type of attention with those around me my business flourishes.

Sometimes I realize I'm not following Father Vincent's example. It is a bad habit that slowly grows. It is easy to justify looking something up quickly on the laptop while listening to a client. I could give them the information immediately, couldn't I? And checking a website or email while talking to my husband – that wasn't too bad was it? It grows to quickly glancing at my email message subjects while a business contact is talking about something I was less than interested in. I may skim my Twitter feed when on the phone. Soon it's just a click to check a message or blog that looks interesting and I'm off reading instead of listening.

If I want to keep my healthy business, it has to stop. If you want a big yield business, you stop multitasking people.

If you truly need to do something else, then let the other person know you'll call them back, talk to them at lunch, or be available at another time. Resist the urge to quickly look something up unless you identify to the other person that you are doing so. Set aside time to do those multitasking duties, and don't interact with people at that time. You will get more accomplished in your business with people when you focus on them and then focus on tasks separately.

Thoughtful Questions:

What distracts you most often when you are on the phone with a business associate?

_____

_____

_____

_____

Have you ever had someone say "good bye" on a call, and you knew it was because you were distracted? How did you feel about it?

_____

_____

_____

_____

Which social media platforms distract you or tempt you to multitask?

_____

_____

_____

_____

What do you think the impact is on your business from multitasking people (not just you, but when your employees or contractors do it)?

_____

_____

_____

_____

When have you seen multitasking give a negative impression?

_____

_____

_____

_____

What is your business' policy on phones in business meetings?

_____

_____

_____

_____

Skillful Practice:

When you are on the phone, minimize all computer windows and turn over any papers you were reading. Only have a piece of paper available for notes. If you are meeting with someone, turn your phone over so you can't see it light up with notifications. Better yet, leave it in your coat pocket/purse or turn it off totally. Set aside specific times in the day to do the "busy work" which you often do while multitasking (like checking emails, responding to social media, checking texts, looking up information.)

Skill #25 - Be open to truth

When communicating in any situation, even work, you need to keep in mind you have your truth and the other person has theirs. This is normal. In speaking you acknowledge verbally it is your truth, and in listening you are trying to understand the other person's truth. But whether you are the speaker or the listener multiple truths are important to keep in mind. Both of you will stay clear.

The following joke recently came across my virtual desk:

At my granddaughter's wedding, the DJ polled the guests to see who had been married longest; it turned out to be my husband and me. The DJ asked us, "What advice would you give to the newly-married couple?" I answered, "The three most important words in a marriage are 'You're probably right'." Everyone then looked at my husband who said, "She's probably right."

You know, a great relationship skill is right out in the open in this joke. However, the message isn't only for marriage. Those three words, "You're probably right," can go miles toward making any relationship work, even a business one.

Just imagine what would happen if people from different political parties started focusing on what is "right" in the others person's message rather than trying to denounce and pick each other apart. And how about using it with a customer who has a complaint about you? What would happen if you took a moment to say "You're probably right; could you tell me more about what you experienced?" What if you were supportive of an employee by telling them they may be right and encouraging them to flesh new ideas they have out? How about saying to your boss "You might be right about that, what can we do about it?"

Fights over "truth" are damaging to business relationships. Everyone has their own filters and how they see things (even you); that doesn't make one more right than the other. For example, when one person has been in an industry for years and the other isn't, they may see problems and solutions from totally different points of view. Both will have a "truth" about what is going on. When you are listening your job is to understand— to see that the other person (boss, coworker, vendor, or customer) has their own truth and it is right for them. It also means you need to own up to what events looks like their truth – even if it is only 5% true.

Dandemis said, *"Do not condemn the judgment of another because it differs from your own. You may both be wrong."* Learn to see at least part of the other side.

One thing that makes it hard to admit the other person may be right is we only see and pay attention to what we think is important (or right), and we ignore or forget the other things. We are constantly filtering the input of the world. This is actually a survival function. If you didn't filter, you'd be overwhelmed and catatonic. (Some theorists suggest this is part of what happens in severe forms of autism.)

What do these filters have to do with business relationships? It means you and the person you are talking with each have your own ways of seeing and understanding things because of your filters. Those filters create each person's truth and what they think is right.

Example – when people learn I'm a therapist they think I'm going to analyze them. I don't try to do it, but there is some truth to their concern. I have a certain way of looking at things which includes trying to figure people out. That's part of who I am; it's what makes me a good therapist and coach.

So, when I'm talking to someone, my husband for example, I have to keep in mind my therapy type filters and be aware of them. I have to make sure I'm communicating **out** through my filters in such a way the information can get **in** through his filters (which are very different than mine, unsurprisingly.) I have to do the same thing while talking to a business colleague or a client, and so do you.

This means you *have to say things in multiple different ways in order to be understood.* It means you need to *acknowledge the other person could be right* in what they say. Trust me; usually the other person is not trying to be difficult; they are communicating through their filters. It is normal, and you have to find ways to get ideas back and forth past the gauntlet of filters.

Once you realize everyone has their own truth influenced by their filters, you have a business edge. You start talking to people in a way that will bypass their filters. You learn how to listen through your filters to get a clearer picture of what is going on. This allows you to respond better and grow a great business.

Thoughtful Questions:

What are your filters? (It may help to look at how you think, what things/attitudes/thoughts you struggle to understand, and what things you may have learned growing up.)

_____

_____

_____

_____

How do you think saying "You may be right about that" more will impact your business?

_____

_____

_____

_____

What do you think you can gain by acknowledging and listening to other peoples' truths in your business?

_____

_____

_____

_____

Skillful Practice:

For the next few days when you are listening work hard to understand the other person's truth. If it seems appropriate, use "you may be right about that" to gather more information and help the other person feel important/recognized. Journal about your experiences. Identify when your own filters get in the way of really hearing another person or speaking to them. Discover ways to recognize when you are getting caught up by your filters.

I believe in giving more to my customers than they expect, so here are a few more skills that you can use to grow your successful business. Three of them are additional skills and the last one is the basis of all other skills.

Bonus Skill #1 - Use Silence

As a therapist, I learned early (before college even) how important silence is for moving people forward. I have lost count of the number of times I just sat quietly and something profound and insightful came out of a client's mouth. It works wonders. Silence can also be a potent skill for your business.

Part of the reason silence is powerful is because it is so rare in this day and age. You are bombarded by information from the moment you get up (and turn on the news or handle the kids or rush out of the house) to the second you return to bed (after setting up coffee, checking that last email, watching the evening news.) Technology keeps up a constant chatter into your brain, and you feel you can't stop it. You are on overload and I bet you don't truly realize it (you think it's natural, or usual.)

What happens, then, when there is silence?

You fill it!! You get busy with something. You start talking. You turn on the television, computer, or video games. You create "noise." In other words, you distract yourself and miss out on the power of a moment of silence.

Silence is tough because you have to sit with your thoughts. You have to acknowledge something your business associate just said. You have to be comfortable with yourself and the person you are with. The opposite, noise, lets you avoid all those things.

Silence is a teacher. The things that come up when you are silent (either alone or in a business interaction) can be wonderful growth opportunities.

Silence is about respect. When something is difficult for a business associate, it is rude to avoid it by getting noisy. Silent acceptance and quiet discussion is called for.

Silence is contemplative. Silence leads you inward rather than distracting you outward. And it is in the inward journey (into yourself, or into your business) where you learn and grow the most.

Silence when used in business meetings can make great ideas come to the forefront. Silence when used while talking to a customer can let them come to a decision to buy. Attentive silence can show respect when a business associate is sharing and gives you a chance to understand (review the early chapter on listening to understand.) Thoughtful silence in a negotiation may encourage the other person to give a little more.

Silence, when used respectfully, can flip the switch for business takeoff.

Thoughtful Questions:

How do you feel when a conversation or meeting has a few moments of silence?

_____

_____

_____

_____

What do you make up or think about silences in meetings and interactions?

_____

_____

_____

_____

Are you comfortable with silences or do you try to fill them, and if so, how?

_____

_____

_____

_____

What things have silences given to your business?

_____

_____

_____

_____

What problems in your business have come from filling the silences?

_____

_____

_____

_____

Skillful Practice:

When someone shares a great idea or intense bit of information, take a long slow breath before replying. Make sure you remain focused on them so they know you are paying attention, but the breath will provide a moment of silence and show respect for what was shared or at least the person sharing. During meetings identify moments of silent contemplation; say something like, "Okay, we've heard all the issues on this topic; let us all take a quiet moment to gather our thoughts before diving in to problem solving." Give your business associates permission to use silence and create an atmosphere of thought and motivation rather than frenetic busy-ness.

Bonus Skill #2 - Getting an A

If you want an employee or customer to do something more often, recognize it, applaud it, and ask for more. You'll get more of what you want by appreciating rather than complaining, by asking instead of assuming.

You should always:

Acknowledge. Make sure you recognize when your customer, employee or business associate does something good or something you like or something you asked them to do. Send a handwritten thank you note (it will surprise them as very few people use snail mail anymore.) What you recognize and focus on will happen again. Would you rather it be the good things like a purchase and good work, or the bad things like sloppy work or returns?

Amplify. Don't just "mention" the good things, *amplify* them. While you give a compliment focus on giving it and having it be received. Take a moment to make sure it sinks in (use silence! See the chapter "Use Silence".) What you say will be better heard and remembered if you do this. Trust me; I use it all the time with clients- it works.

Apologize. If you make a mistake, own up to it and apologize. Don't avoid it and act like it didn't happen. Don't wait to be caught. Stand up for all your decisions and apologize. Make sure to not ruin your apology with an excuse "I'm sorry, but an employee came in late." (By the way, see how that sentence also has "but" in it – double whammy!) Remember, apologies aren't just about words. If you say "I'm sorry," but your attitude is "get over it" you aren't really apologizing. Your remorse needs to be tangible. The better you are at appropriate apologies the more customer retention you will have and the happier your employees will be.

Articulate. Open your mouth and speak your truth, no matter how uncomfortable that is for you. Don't stuff your needs or your thoughts- you aren't being fair to your business associates if you aren't being you. Take time to think about what you say and how you say it so you can articulate yourself clearly rather than confuse others. But make sure you say what you need to say. (Remember the chapters on making requests and how to share?)

Ask. Talk about what you want, what you like, what you don't like- and *ask* your business associate to help with these things. Ask for help and be willing to receive it. Ask the questions you want answers to. Ask what your business contact is thinking. If you want to know what they are thinking about you- ask that. Make sure you are clear with your questions, too.

There are a few ways business people fumble their compliments. Do you do any of these?

1. You hide your compliments in subtlety. Let's face it, your business partner may miss the "that was a great idea" look, you need to say it out loud, directly.

2. You mistakenly give a compliment between two complaints. That's backward; sandwich a suggestion between two positives.

3. You overpower your employee with negatives. You talk about all the things you are unhappy about, what they are doing wrong, and then expect them to hear a nice word or two.

4. You get overwhelmed and forget. You get caught up in your own life, worries, and fears, and forget you are part of a team, even if the team is you and your customers. Reaching out and saying something nice takes you out of that negativity.

5. You worry if you compliment your employee or vendor for working on something, they'll "slack off." Not true; compliments only encourage.

6. You just don't know what to say or worry it'll come out wrong. The worst thing you can do is say nothing, so say something nice.

All of these are really just excuses. Giving a compliment or apologizing means being aware. It means catching someone doing something good and owning up when you make a mistake. It takes a little work, but it reaps great business benefits. When people feel good about your business and you in it, they will help out.

Thoughtful Questions:

Which of the "A"s do you struggle with? (Acknowledge, Amplify, Apologize, Articulate, Ask) Why?

_____

_____

_____

_____

What thoughts do you have about compliments and apologies in business? (For example, I had one client who believed that adults "shouldn't" need acknowledgement, "That's just for kids.")

_____

_____

_____

_____

How do you respond to compliments?

_____

_____

_____

_____

How do you think your reaction to/feelings about compliments impacts your ability to give them?

_____

_____

_____

_____

How are you at apologizing? Do you do it immediately or wait? (Hint: the more immediate the apology the better for your business.)

_____

_____

_____

_____

Skillful Practice:

For the next week send out an email or card a day thanking someone who has done something for you or your business. Spell out what you appreciated and make sure you say thank you clearly. Don't ask for anything, just say thank you. Additionally, if you have someone who needs an apology from your or your business, either make a call or handwrite a personal apology offering a sorry and a suggestion how you can make it better in some way.

Bonus Skill #3 - Small Steps and Simple Rules

I've been cleaning my office the last few beautiful days. It feels so good to get organized and freshened up!

Why don't I maintain it between-times? Maybe I'm just human? I get lax, stop doing, and forget organization.

In her lovely book, "<u>Comfort Living</u>", Christine Eisner shares six succinct tips for tending your space:

- If you open it, close it
- If you put it down, pick it up
- If you take it off, hang it up
- If you mess it up, clean it up
- If you take it out, put it back

She notes, "You will be clearing a path that makes it easier to enjoy the small pleasures and relaxing moments that make a good life." Often it is the small simple rules like these that you follow that make things go smoothly and wonderfully.

Give a thought to what you can be doing to tend your business relationships. Implement a list of rules like these:

- If something needs to be done, do it
- If you want something, ask for it
- If you like something, appreciate it
- If you feel unsupported, reach out
- If you see a need, fill it
- If a customer has an expectation, exceed it

You can post your rules where everyone in your business sees and follows them.

Look at the things you want to change or cleanup in your business. At the minimum you should be doing regular business checkups and cleanups. Look at what is working and what isn't. Throw out any damaging behaviors or procedures that have crept in; spruce up and reinforce the successful things you are doing. Clean up files, close up open jobs, send out thank you notes, and make a to-do list.

And hopefully that refreshing, relaxing, and complete feeling will stay around your business most of the year.

Thoughtful Questions:

How do you "get behind" on the maintenance of your business relationships?

_____

_____

_____

_____

What things do you put off, dislike doing, or resent?

_____

_____

_____

_____

What change can you implement to make sure these things get done in a timely way? (For example, I identified the last business day of the month as an organization day, and I schedule nothing else that day.)

_____

_____

_____

_____

What are the "simple rules" in your business (good or bad) and how would you like to change them?

_____

_____

_____

_____

Skillful Practice:

Take out your journal and set a timer for 10 minutes. Writing the whole time, brainstorm the organizational rules for yourself and your business. Not just the "If you do ____, do____" things, but what would you like done regularly so your business keeps running smoothly. Think of what you are avoiding, too, and include those things. When you are done, look at your writing and make a to-do list.

Fundamental Skill - Respect

Ultimately, all the skills you have read about are based in respect. Without respect you will fail at each and every one of the skills in this book. Without respect, your business will remain on the ground and not grow toward the sky. Respect is the basis for all healthy growth in both the personal and professional arenas.

Respect is a privilege, not a right or a due. It is something you give to others and expect from them. It is also something you give to yourself and create in your business.

When you are respectful it teaches others how to respect you. Throughout my childhood and teen years my friends always respected my mother, no matter how disrespectful I knew them to be in other situations. I never questioned it; it was just natural. When I look back I realize that attitude toward my mother (actually both of my parents) came about because my mother unfailingly treated all of my friends with respect, and she expected the same in return. My friends who did the worst cursing at school never cursed more than once in front of my mom. She'd look at them and calmly say, "There is no speaking like that in this house," my friend would apologize, and my mother would smile acceptingly. That friend would then never swear in front of my mother again.

How others treat you (and how you allow them to treat you) are two areas of respect you need to nurture. There is no relationship without respect - business, friendship, family, or acquaintance. Respect is based on understanding limits and boundaries in a relationship. It comes from you knowing yourself and your business and being able to communicate that to customers, partners, employees, and vendors. When respect is working it feels like a win-win, or a good give and take. And as you express it to the people who are in contact with your business, you decide if they are acting with respect and being healthy for your company.

However, if you don't respect yourself and your business, there is no way you can expect your customers and vendors to respect them. Laurence Sterne said *"Respect for ourselves guides our morals; respect for others guides our manners."*

You have to understand what you think, what you feel, and how you act. You deserve to be respectful in and of all three of these things. When you act disrespectfully it doesn't feel good in the long term, nor does it build a strong company. If you have disrespectful thoughts, it comes across in your attitude and actions, negatively impacting your business. When you don't respect your feelings, you make poor decisions for your business.

Additionally, you deserve to be respected. Honestly, if I had a friend who refused to respect my Mom, I am not sure she would have welcomed them back to the house. I'm quite sure I wouldn't have. In fact, there was one couple who came to a get together who were never invited back (nor to any of my other friends' houses) after they were blatantly disrespectful of not only my parents but the others at the party. That's what happens when you don't respect yourself enough to be respectful to others.

Respect of your business flows from your understanding of your business. If you did buy and complete Mike Mikalowitz's book, you'll have a list of the limits of your business in your immutable laws. Respect is a core law in my business. Hopefully from the work you've done in this book you'll better understand the purpose of your business.

Respect is shown through appreciation and recognition. When you use compliments you show respect. When you ask "How can I help you?" you are recognizing your customer as someone who may have a need. Respect also is about recognizing excellence. Recognize it in yourself, and even more so, affirm it in customers, vendors, and employees. Affirm it loudly. My mother used to say "Are you at least jumping up and down inside" when she'd get a

"That was good" for a comment about something she did well. She knew how important it was to make the celebration big.

Just so we are clear, there are some things respect is not. It is not critical. Constructive criticism rarely is constructive, nor respectful. Instead try brainstorming with the person what they could do differently. Or make a request for a change in their behavior without criticizing or berating them. Respect is also not disdainful – it does not come from a one-up position, only an equal stance on the same level. It is not neglectful. Respect is about paying attention and catching yourself and other people doing well so you can esteem them. Lastly, it is never abusive or sarcastic. If you believe "I'm just being myself" when you are either of these things, then you have missed the point of the skills presented in this book.

Respect in every interaction makes your work flourish. As long as all the skills you use are done in an attitude of respect, you cannot do them "wrong" and you will grow a great business.

Thoughtful Questions:

In what areas do you let yourself be less than respectful? Why do you feel it is okay at those times?

_____

_____

_____

_____

When has lack of respect caused trouble for you or your business?

_____
_____
_____
_____

What does it feel like to you when someone disrespects you? Do you fall into disrespecting them (and by extension yourself)?

_____
_____
_____
_____

How can you keep yourself respectful even when someone is acting disrespectfully toward you or your business?

_____
_____
_____
_____

Which of the skills in this book do you think relate most to respect? Which ones, if not practiced, could be seen as disrespect?

_____
_____
_____
_____

Skillful Practice:

Go buy a package of blank greeting cards. Whenever a vendor does something special for your business, send them a note of thank you, and outline exactly what they did that you appreciate and how it helped. When you see a customer has a special happening (for example you see they are getting a reward, or that they are now the president of an organization, or that they are now at 5 years with their current company) send them a card of congratulations. [If you are asking how you will know these things, it would behoove you to get on LinkedIn and connect with customers!] When an employee goes out of their way to do something extra or they do an exceptional job on something, give them a card outlining what they did, why it was great, and saying they are appreciated.

If you struggle to stay respectful when someone is disrespectful to you, take some time to journal ideas on how you can hold yourself in a healthy space despite their bad behaviors. Brainstorm ways you can respectfully disconnect from disrespectful behaviors. Review all the skills in this book to see which ones you think you can use in these types of situations.

Practice the skills in this book; all of them show respect!

In Conclusion – Some Lessons from Baseball

You may read about many of the skills outlined in this book and be tempted to say "That's not me" or "I've never been able to _____ (listen, deal with conflict, understand others, etc.)" or "I'm not a _____ (empathetic, verbose, patient, etc.) person." All of those things may be true, but only up to a point. You may never have been those things ... before now. Why? Because you have not learned and regularly practiced the skills.

Everything in this book is about skill building, not about changing your personality. You are not doing these things to change who you are; you are studying these skills to improve yourself in business (and maybe in your personal relationships too.) You are learning, practicing and mastering the skills to the best of your ability. You may not be an expert in them, but you sure as heck can learn how to use them.

Let me give you an example. If I asked you if you are a professional baseball player, most of you would say "No." (If you are a professional baseball player reading this book, let me know, I'm curious! And then substitute a different skill in this story, please.) When you say "No, I'm not a professional baseball player" you are probably right; however, that doesn't preclude you from learning how to play baseball. You might practice enough to play in local recreation leagues, or with your friends, or to throw and bunt the ball with your kid in the park. You learn those baseball skills to the level you want and to the best of your ability. Not all of us are built or born to be a professional level athlete, but that doesn't keep you from learning the skills to a proficient level.

So, instead of saying "I'm not" say "I can." I can learn these skills. I can practice these skills. I can use these skills to best express who I am, what I want, and to cultivate my business.

Here's to not just owning your business, but to growing it and reaping a great harvest!

~~~~~~

Thank you for reading my book!

If you enjoyed it, please
take a quick moment to rate it on Amazon.

And don't forget to go to
eepurl.com/bU_Jdj
for your bonus
"Common Mistakes People Make in Communication."